What are others saying about Jeffrey Dobkin's information-rich, conversational style of writing and his small business marketing and direct marketing advice? <u>Unsolicited</u> comments—

"Your book, How To Market a Product for Under $500, *is one of the best books I've ever read on how to market a product."*
    E. Joseph Cossman

"We doubled the weight of your book: We underlined the important parts!"

"We recommended your book to some friends, and decided to put yellow sticky notes in the pages we especially wanted them to read. Several hundred sticky notes later we abandoned the idea, and finally just bought them their own copy, and told them to read the whole thing."

"I can't give you enough gratitude for writing this book. I've learned more about real-life business in three days than I did in 41/2 years of college."

"A much-needed book, very well done."
    Dan Poynter, author of The Self-Publishing Manual

"Your book presents a unique blend of traditional and guerilla marketing techniques in an unpretentious, user-friendly format. What a refreshing change of pace from the stacks of trade mags, newsletters and "how-to" books that clutter my office. I found dozens of pragmatic and affordable suggestions to share with my clients!"
    Henry Berkowitz, President, HB Publishing and Marketing

"I've read just about every book ever written on copy; you definitely belong in the copywriter's hall of fame. Your book is must *reading for any serious seller of goods or services."*

"If an inventor is not sure whether licensing or distributing is the way to go, this book could be his bible. Dobkin cuts through months or years of doing it by trial and error."
    Don Costar, Nevada Inventor's Association Newsletter

"Definitely the best book on marketing I have ever read! I only wish I had read it years ago. It would have saved me many years and thousands of dollars. It is must *reading..."*

"I ordered your amazing book..."

"Just wanted to tell you again that your book is the best marketing book for small business that I know, and I've read a bunch of them. Terrific, terrific book."

"I've read most of the articles, and even though I am the Director of Marketing for a national association, I must say, I learned something from every one."

"I find your writing to be clear, free of jargon, and full of useful information. You're my kind of writer. Of course, as an old hand with more than 40 years in advertising, I feel like I can be a good judge of the content of your work. Thank you for letting me publish your writing."
     Don R. Blum, Publisher, Savannah Business Journal

"Useful for the author with a book to promote, as well as for the writer who prepares marketing materials for clients." Freelance Writer's Report

"I got your book at the library—they wanted it back. Enclosed is my check..."

"I kept your book out [of the library] so long it would have been cheaper to buy it right from the start."

"I must again compliment you on the detailed thoroughness of your book. There are other books on the subject matter, but they lack the step-by-step panache of yours. Your coverage of the press release was excellent...and I had every confidence in talking to the writer. Thanks to you I must have sounded like I knew what I was talking about. I asked all the right questions."

"When I first read one of your articles, I was impressed by your expertise and your thoroughness. Your telephone consultation and book, How To Market a Product for Under $500!, *were invaluable to me in the process of developing our direct mail program."*

"Your book is wonderful...full of insightful and practical information...has already more than paid for itself...look forward to using your book as reference for years to come."

"This is by far the best book I have ever read on the topics of direct marketing and mail order sales. Well-researched and organized...the book's coverage is exhaustive."

"Again, your section on press releases is great. Have it almost memorized."

"I've been enthusiastically recommending it to anyone who'll listen."

"I was amazed that I could actually start marketing my ideas with a low budget. Your book is beyond excellent. I have read many other marketing books, such as the series by so-called guru XXXXXX. Your book makes XXXXX look like he needs to get a copy, and start studying....Your book has taught me more than I could have ever imagined (and even more than my friends that graduated with business degrees)."

"An excellent resource for ideas on how to sell your products and services inexpensively."

~ AUTHOR'S NOTE ~

WITH THIS BOOK I HAVE TRIED TO MAKE IT POSSIBLE FOR PEOPLE TO UNDERSTAND WHAT MARKETING IS AND DOES, THEN BE ABLE TO ACCOMPLISH THIS MARKETING FUNCTION WITHOUT ADDITIONAL HELP.

FURTHER, I HAVE TRIED TO GO DEEP INTO ADVANCED MARKETING TECHNIQUES FOR THE SAVVY MARKETER AND PERHAPS OFFER HIM OR HER THAT ONE GREAT IDEA THEY BOUGHT THIS BOOK FOR... IN EACH CHAPTER.

THROUGHOUT, I ENCOURAGE INVENTORS, PRODUCT DEVELOPERS, PRODUCT MANAGERS, DIRECT MERCHANTS, MARKET MANAGERS, & BUSINESS OWNERS TO FIND THEIR MARKETS EFFICIENTLY AND WITH SPEED, THEN REACH THEM AT THE LOWEST COST.

IT IS A PRIVILEGE TO BE ABLE TO SHARE MY MARKETING KNOWLEDGE AND EXPERTISE WITH MY FELLOW ENTREPRENEURS AND FRIENDS. THANK YOU FOR THIS OPPORTUNITY.

Direct Marketing Strategies
Reference: Marketing, Direct Marketing, New Product Marketing, Sales, Small Business, Product Development, Inventing, Brand Marketing, Multiple Exposure Marketing

While due care has been exercised in the compilation of this marketing manual, we are not responsible for errors or omissions. Inclusion in this guide does not constitute endorsement or recommendation by the publisher unless stated otherwise. These references are intended to assist in providing information to the public, and the information is delivered as accurately as possible.

~ DIRECT MARKETING STRATEGIES ~
JEFFREY DOBKIN

To my good friend,
~ Marc Berk ~
a very clever guy & a
great inventor!

Jeffrey Dobkin

BOOKS
THEY'RE EVERYTHING
YOU'VE EVER IMAGINED...
AND MORE!

DANIELLE ADAMS
PUBLISHING COMPANY

Direct Marketing Strategies
by Jeffrey Dobkin

Published by
— The Danielle Adams Publishing Company —
Box 100
Merion Station, PA 19066
Telephone 610/642-1000
Fax 610/642-6832

Printed and Bound in the United States of America
— Printed on Acid-Free Paper —

Disclaimer: While due care has been taken in the printing of this book, we are not responsible for typographical errors, misspellings, errors in addition, subtraction, multiplication and especially division; names, pricing, locations and so forth which may have occurred, because sometimes this stuff just gets out. Sometimes we misspell words on purpose to see if you'd notice. Or so that picky people have something to complain about. There, see how nice we are? And maybe the names have been changed to protect the innocent? While we'd like to accept responsibility, we don't. In fact, we are not responsible for any-thing. Please buy this book as we may need someone to blame. We can then point to you and say - you read it last and it was your responsibility. We didn't say it was actually your fault, we just said we were going to blame you. Thanks.

The opinions in this text are not necessarily those of the publisher. Or the author. We're not really sure whose they are. Please see our full disclaimer on page 222 or 233 or somewhere around there in the back of the book. Thank you.

~ DIRECT MARKETING STRATEGIES ~

Table of Contents, continued:

We hope you enjoy this book and find it of great value.

To my oldest and dearest friend, and also My Brother

~ **Dean Dobkin** ~

We've been through a lot, Dean and I.

Lately, Dean has been through much more of "a lot" than I. So this dedication is to reaffirm what he has always known, that to me — outside of my own wife and children — you and our brother Bob are absolutely the most cared for individuals in my life. You have always been there for me, and it is a privilege to be here for you. Whenever you need me, just call.

~ DIRECT MARKETING STRATEGIES ~
JEFFREY DOBKIN

Welcome...

THE 23 BEST
LINES IN MARKETING

Like old friends, these lines are of great value to have at your side. This reoccurring arsenal of words is a center point in almost all of my campaigns.

In Direct Mail:

"Gift Certificate Enclosed"

The best envelope teaser copy ever. How many times have I said this? Whew. My very favorite line for getting my clients' direct mail packages opened. The reasons?

- Gift certificates are inexpensive to print, at 1/3rd or 1/4 of a sheet of paper - or less.

- May be printed on the same sheet as the letter, catalog or the order form - for extra savings in printing costs.

- Ship flat, and adds very little weight to your mailing package.

- They're much more upscale than coupons.

- Gift certificates have a high perceived value.

- Cheap to redeem - in fact, have no cost at all until redemption.

- May be targeted to specific merchandise or offers - good for overstock or high margin items.

- Naturally easy to track.

Any arguments?

"Free Offer Inside..."

Works almost as well. When a gift certificate just won't suffice in a business-to-business mailing, this is usually my next choice. And more often than not, the other writing on the envelope is:

"OPEN IMMEDIATELY!"

There's a saying around here in Direct Mailville that states you must tell the recipient exactly what you want him to do for the best chance of having him do exactly what you want.

"Just Call and Get...

How many times have I said this phrase? Hummm, nope, can't count that high. I mix it in with one of my other key phrases:

"Call Us TOLL FREE..."

In a copywriting assignment for an envelope printer, I asked readers to call 16 times in a 2 page letter. 16 times in one letter! So don't feel bad about asking customers to call three or four times on the same page. If you'd like to see how I weaved this into the letter copy without being too obnoxious, just drop me a note and I'll send you the letter. Yes, the letter definitely made his phone ring.

"Dear Colleague"

It's one of my favorite salutations. So much better than 'Dear reader,' which is always my last choice. And who's to say your reader isn't a colleague in some fashion.

"...and Friend."

I like to offer this phrase after the salutation, to make it friendlier and more personal. And it does. "Dear fellow Pharmacist and Friend". "Dear Pet Lover and Friend". "Dear Chevy Owner and Friend". About 50% of my letters have these two words after the opening salutation. In any type of local mailing, my favorite opening is "Dear Neighbor and Friend". Sounds kinda' nice, n'est-ce pas? Readers usually think so, too.

"Thank You."

You know, you can never say 'thank you' enough to your customers. Never. Almost every letter I send has the word thanks in it at one point. Another way I express this is:

"Thank you for your business, and your trust."

If you don't thank them, how are your customers to know you care, or appreciate their business? Chances are they won't. That means if they have the opportunity to go elsewhere, they will. I ran monthly advertising with a magazine for 6 years, they never thanked me once in a letter. When the ad became marginal, I dropped out, and never felt one bit of remorse, despite their pleas. Contrast this to the form we shipped our product with: our shipping form measured 4-1/2" x 7-1/2", and I thanked our customer 6 times on this form. You can call me on this one too, just drop a note and ask for our old Merion Station Mail Order shipping form. Thanks.

"Thank you for your kind referral."

One of the best ways to get business is through referrals. One of the best ways to get more referrals is to send a thank you letter to the person who made a referral. No, a phone call is not the same. When you hang up after a phone conversation you cease to exist. A letter, well, that can hang around for a while - to be appreciated over time. I once wrote a nice 'thank you' letter to a retailer who installed my car radio. They framed it and hung it on their wall - for about a year.

Face it, when someone calls to say thanks, you say "That's nice, they called." End of story. But when you receive a letter of thanks... well, that's big time. Someone actually took the time to sit down and write a letter of thanks. Wow, monumental effort. They know you appreciate it. To our firm, a referral means someone gave our name with the silent pledge of their trust. It is an honor we don't take lightly.

"Thank you for the opportunity and the privilege to be of service."

Business rule number one: it is a privilege to serve your customer. Let them know this is how you feel, and customers will remain loyal to you for years. Not only do I say this frequently, I believe it. So does every person in our firm - it is part of our company creed.

DIRECT MARKETING STRATEGIES

"New Product Offers Benefit!"

This formula is unusual in that it works almost every-where. In direct mail, it's a safe bet for envelope teaser copy, especially when coupled with the three great lines at the top of this article. "New product offers benefit" also is one of the best, time tested formula for the headline of ad, or a press release headline.

It's also my very favorite formula for the "Jeff Dobkin Ben-efits-First Press Release." I've found if you use this formula for the first line of your press release the benefits never, ever get cut out. Editors cut from the bottom, and sometimes from the middle, but the first sentence is always left intact. Since benefits sell the product and increase the response, it's a hard-hitting direct marketing technique to squeeze them in anywhere you can. They'll look just great up at the top of your press release.

"Free Booklet offers how-to information."

This headline attracts readers with a free offer, but also limits the attraction to the specific market segment you are targeting to better qualify respondents. This saves you time, and money by not having to send literature to a non-buying, poor-prospect market. On the upside: "Free booklet shows you how to pack glassware for moving!" produces good re-sponse, but only from people who are going to move. Very targeted marketing. This type of headline produces tons of high quality, highly qualified leads.

"Objective:"

Before writing any copy, including sales letters, brochures, direct mail packages, catalogs, everything - first write "Objec-tive:" in the upper right hand part of a clean sheet of paper. Then write the objective. I do this at the start of every writing assignment. This reminds me why I am writing, and what the writing must accomplish. Unless I'm drafting a catalog or hard hitting package that sells products directly, my objective is usually to make the phone ring; so my copy is written to sell the phone call. Objective: to make the customer pick up the phone and call.

16

Writing the objective first, clarifies my writing. The objective is usually a surprise to most of my business-to-business clients who think I am trying to sell their products. Heck, it's tough to sell from a sheet of paper. I generally leave the selling to them. I just make the phone ring - with warmed-up prospects.

In PR: "Are you the person I should send this press release to?"

I don't think I've ever met an editor who isn't incredibly sick and tired of press agents or product developers who call up and say, "Did you get my press release?" Sure they got your press release. They receive all the press releases - which one was yours? This is usually followed by a flurry of activity: the editor having to fumble through the stacks of papers, half-written stories, half-finished coffee, and occasionally toward the deadline of the month — half-eaten pizzas — sitting on their desk to find your release. I guarantee by the time they found it, your press release has one foot in the grave - er... wastebasket. Still in all, more likely than not, you're going to have to send another press release to make sure they have it on-hand and at the ready.

Yet it's much more likely your press release will be published if you speak with an editor. So here's the plan: Call the editor BEFORE sending him or her a press release, and ask, "Are you the person I should send this press release to?" You see, this sets up a 'can you help me' relationship with the editor, and editors by their nature - like school teachers - are a very helpful lot. If they say yes, give them a short, one minute pitch (they're also a very busy lot) and then send your release to them. This will increase your chance of being published from 5% to 50%, maybe 70%, maybe 80%.

If the editor isn't the right one, and says "Oh no, you've got to send that to Jeff Rogers, our chief editor down the hall." You then pick up the phone and knowing full well Rogers is the one, you call and say to him. "Are you the person I should send this release to..." You see, this sets up a 'can you help me' relationship...

"Nice speaking with you."

Even if it wasn't, "Nice speaking with you, thank you for receiving my call." should be the first line of the letter you include with the press release that you send to an editor after you've spoken with him or her. (Yes, I believe all press releases should be sent with a letter). Since most press releases are sent without phone calls, this subtly reminds the editor of your conversation, and that the publishing of this particular release has great importance to you. Also remember not to say in your letter, "Enclosed is our release..." they can see that. Instead, your letter focus should be on "Thank you so much for your consideration to publish our release. Your readers will get this wonderful informational booklet, shipped promptly, filled with terrific ideas and tips on...". Letters with press releases build your credibility.

"See Page..."

In catalogs I always like to refer customers to other pages. Whether it's accessories, similar items, or just stuff that goes well with other stuff, the best thing a customer can do is thumb through the pages. The longer the customer stays in your book, the better the chance he'll order something, or order something else.

"See Order Form on Page..."

If the objective is to have customers order, it never hurts to remind them. Pointing to the order for is a subtle re-minder. A nice phrase is "It's easy to order - see Order Form on page..."

"What's New Inside..."

In newsletters, catalogs, long copy packages, and other longer publications I like to entice readers with a bulleted list of fascinating places to go to inside. If we can just spike a couple of high interest notes and get the reader inside, we've accomplished the cover objective and have a good start toward our goals of additional time in our package and increasing sales and brand loyalty.

"And how did you hear of our company?"

Built into every advertising and marketing program should be a tracking system. When your marketing is purely through the mail it may be easy to track through a priority code number, response sent to a particular department, or simply a color coded envelope. But some marketing programs, and most retail operations need to figure out which ad their customer saw or which offer they are responding to. I always recommend this simple method: leave a small pad of paper or stack of 3" x 5" index cards next to each phone, and when it rings - early in the conversation - ask "And how did you hear of our company?"

Take all the filled-out slips of paper and put them in a selected drawer. At the end of the month you'll have a good idea which ad or program is working. At the end of 6 months you'll know for sure which ads were profitable and which mailing worked the best.

"It's a little over, is that OK?"

OK, so it isn't used in direct mail. But I don't know of a deli counter man this side of New York who hasn't used this up-selling line at least a thousand times a week. Pretty effective marketing, eh?

"Satisfaction Always Guaranteed"

Heck, you're going to get stuck with it anyhow if it comes back, might as well be a nice guy and say this right up front. It'll increase your sales.

"Kindest regards,"

I sign off of every letter this way. Kinda' nice, don't you think?

USING INCENTIVES TO INCREASE SALES

I LOVE TRADE SHOWS. I've never gone to a trade show where I didn't have a great time. And, at least it's a day out of the office. You know what they say: a lousy day on the golf course is better than a good day in the office. Hummm - I wonder if the florescent lighting has anything to do with my ADHD? I just got a new game on my computer and it's... hey, nice shirt you're wearing, where'd you get it?

A few of the best trade shows of the entire year are in the incentive industry, also called the rewards and motivation industry. These are the shows that cross all industry boundaries; manufacturers of all types offer their products as business gifts to reward salespeople, dealers, distributors, and customers. Let's see... did I leave anybody out? No, guess not.

One east coast tradition is the Incentive Show (www. theincentiveshow.com), held every spring at the Jacob Javits Convention Center in New York. This year was May 3rd and 4th. Over 200 booths of incentive merchandise and travel. Sign up for free at their website until April 5; after that you'll have to call them and sweet talk them out of the $30 registration fee. Each exhibitor usually gets tons of free passes so if you're late for registration you might try hocking one of these firms.

Even more popular - and larger - is the Motivation Show (www.motivationshow.com) in the fall - usually in late September or early October, in Chicago. This year it's September 26 - 28th, at McCormick place. Over 2100 exhibitors and over 267,640 square feet of exhibit space - this show is huge. I love walking this show - it's endless. Premiums, ad specialties, incentive travel and a whole section of foreign countries incentives and travel.

The reason these shows are so much fun is that the merchandise mix they showcase spans dozens of different industries.

Sure, you can go to an electronics show and see TVs and stereos. You can go to an auto show and see the newest cars. You can go to an adult show and see, well, if your wife doesn't catch you, you can see most anything a man, a woman, a midget, another woman, two sheep, and a duck can do in the privacy of your own hotel room. Just don't get caught walking the sheep through the lobby like I did, er... I mean a friend of mine did. Yea, then try explaining that to the hotel manager. Or to your wife. Or, as we now say, ex-wife. The words, "I can explain." only go so far. Then you have to come up with the explanation. If you just keep repeating that phrase it doesn't really count. In court.

Most trade shows are narrowly focused in one or two primary industries. But the motivational and incentive shows have thousands of products from TV's to automobiles, to camping equipment to cheap imprinted items, er... "promotional products" as we now call them, to expensive pens to trips to luggage to clocks to... well you name it.

Here's how the incentive industry works. If you want a TV, hey, buy it at a retail store. But if you have 100 sales people out on the road and want them to sell, sell, sell, more more more... you offer them an incentive. This may be a new TV, a trip, a car, a lap dance with your ex-wife... what ever. You thought I didn't know. Hey, you're the one that told her to get a job.

So you say to your sales team, "The first 10 people who make this quota next month get a new 56" Sony TV!" Your sales people will gripe about how it ain't possible, the goal is too high, the market is down; but the few at the top will get the message and go to work: they'll sandbag. It's amazing how imaginative you can get if you need to turn in this months sales figures in next months quota.

Here's where the show comes in: you don't buy these 10 TVs from a retailer - you go directly to Sony's Premium Division booth at the show. Tell them you'd like to offer TVs to each of your 100 sales people as an incentive... and their premium division guys - with their eyes wide open - will quote you an amazingly low wholesale price for 100, 56-inch TVs. Then you tell them nah, it's too much $$$. But now that you know what their bottom line is on 56-inch TVs, tell them you'll buy ten at that price. They'll reluctantly agree. Then they'll go in the back room and celebrate, too. Hey - a $25,000 sale is a $25,000 sale.

And frankly, it's a nice way for them to skirt their retail distribution methods without the guys at Best Buy and Circuit City getting mad at them. It's through their premium division that they don't get in trouble with their retailers for selling directly to a customer at a huge discounted price. Yet, they still get the direct sale. You get a better price. Everybody happy. You're happy. Your sales team happy. Sony people happy. Everybody jammin'. I'm jammin' too.

Upscale incentives like TVs, phones, cameras, stereos, and leather make great dealer incentives. A client of mine offers FREE Land's End Sweaters to all purchasers who spend over $2,000 in October. In the summer they offer free lawn chairs, rafts and floats. Seasonal offerings keep dealers talking and the costs are more than offset by the larger purchases.

Promotional products include all kinds of luggage and leather goods, china and silverware, food gifts, clocks and watches, gift cards (very hot right now), clothes and incentive travel. Travel incentives are very common in lots of industries - just ask your insurance agent about all their junkets, perks and free trips for going over their quota. The free trip almost makes it worth it to sell insurance. Of course there's a down side: you go away with 500 other insurance salespeople. Ugh.

We use Cross Pens as business gifts here at our own offices. It's our policy that when someone refers a client to us, I have a Cross pen engraved with their name on it and send it to them with a nice letter of "Thanks for the referral." I figure if I send a Cross pen with my name on it it goes in a drawer - I'm the only person who wants that. With their name engraved on it, it goes in their shirt pocket or in their pocketbook. It's a nice gift. I buy a couple of dozen Cross pens each year and hope one day I'll get a referral. Sigh...

Find Promotional Products at trade shows

So walk around the incentive shows. Lots of giveaways at these shows: this is where manufacturers of giveaways and traffic builders display their products. You know, the cheap stuff that you gave away at the trade shows where you exhibited last year.

Oh, excuse me... the term is now "promotional products," to dress them up so people don't call them "the cheap stuff that you gave away." They're low-cost, but they're incentives just the same. I call them souvenirs. My kids call them "presents". I tell my kids I bought "Dad's special presents!" for them. Shhh. They still believe in Santa and the tooth fairy, too. College kids today just aren't as smart as when we went. Hey, wait a minute. You don't think they're just telling me that to get the presents, do you?

So if you have kids and are looking for these "gifts", then first look for the booth that is giving away the nicest shopping bags and get several. If you are a collector of tsakstsakas, bring a comfortable backpack, too. The serious collectors bring duffel bags.

The ASI Show of the Advertising Specialty Institute, Langhorn, PA (www.ASIShow.com) has more tsakstsakas than anyone (yea, I know it isn't spelled correctly... you try looking it up in a dictionary!). The ASI is the original 8,000 pound gorilla of the ad specialty market. They rule roost of the low end, privately labeled promotional industry items with a firm hand - making money from both sides of the fence:

manufacturers and distributors. They have shows throughout the year but the larger ones are at McCormick place July 11 to 13 this year, and in Philadelphia May 23 - 25th.

The ASI shows are harder to get into unless you are clever, or pay them, or both. But surely you can pick up more cheap pens here than at any other show. You can also pick up thousands of things for the kids, and your office staff, who seem to like the same stuff as the kids and are generally more thankful for being remembered although usually more miffed that you didn't take them.

You just missed one of the best shows but if you register now you'll be very early for it next January 4 - 6 in Las Vegas 2007. It's the PPAI, Promotional Products Association International (www.PPA.Org) show. Each year over 1,600 suppliers exhibit in over 3,700 booths. Lots of giveaways here, too. Remember? "Promotional products." "Advertising specialties." "Cheap stuff you give away." Are they really just synonymous? Wow, nice word, isn't it. Yea, that's right - I know some big words. Don't get smart with me or I'll defenistrate you. Attendance? 23,000.

OK, you're still in luck - the next PPAI trade show, although smaller, is in Atlantic City June 5, 6 & 7 at the conventions center. The PPAI is a non-profit governing association of the promotional products industry. 825 Companies, 1200 booths, with 5,000 distributor attendees. Call them at 888-426-7724 for a list of their services and show information. (It's trade only, so you'll need the know the secret handshake which is, er... ten dollars).

Amongst the highlights of products at any of these shows are flashlights (my personal favorites), key fobs, and the absolute best product is a funny sign flip-book like the one found on my website www.dobkin.com with over 100 funny signs that stands up on your desk and says things like, "I didn't say it was your fault, I said I was going to blame you..."! Oh, did I mention you can buy one for $ 12.95 + $4 Shipping. OK, so I plugged my new book. So? Call 610-642-1000 to order - I need the money.

While you're calling around to the associations, don't forget the IMA, the Incentive Marketing Association (www. incentivemarketing.org) in beautiful downtown Naperville, IL. Population 128,358. Y'all can phone them up at 630-369-7880. (I don't think they get 800 phone service down there yet.) It's the main association of the premium industry.

Besides the shows, there are also a few trade magazines that go to the incentive industry. The oldest is Incentive Marketing; man, this publication was around when I was a kid. You remember those days - we still had records, 33-1/3s, 45s and some were even 78s; cars were all American made... and so was everything else, and there was no Internet. Wow am I really that old? You remember 78s? Wow, you are too.

Incentive Marketing (www.Incentivemag.com) is digest size, glossy, thick and perfect bound. It contains a range of ads from tiny personalized items to full incentive companies that will come in and set up your whole program for you for free just to get the merchandise orders.

Well established and well accepted as one of only two or three magazines that underserves this huge market, the dominance of articles explain how successful incentive programs are run by companies, with a little bit of industry gossip to keep the industry buzzing.

Incentive Marketing magazine, as most trade magazines, is easy to get for free if you know how to pitch them. Their number is 646-654-7654. If you don't know how to get free subscriptions to magazines just request my free article, "Getting Free Trade Magazines." Simply jot your name and address on the back of a twenty dollar bill and send to Jeff Dobkin, P.O. Box 100, Merion Station, PA 19066. OK, a fiver will do, too. Might as well order all my marketing books and programs while you're at it.

Still interested in reading up? Another glossy magazine, Potentials in Marketing, now simply called Potentials, (phone 646-654-5000, www.potentialsmag.com) is tabloid-sized and strictly product oriented. It's a fast-read and fun if you like press releases and product shots. Hey remember comic books? You really are old, aren't you?

Not to be outdone, Promo magazine (www.promomagazine.com) 203-358-9900, has their own show at the Chicago Navy Pier Sept. 30 - Oct. 2nd, in case you didn't get enough free pens from the going to the other shows.

And finally, if you haven't found it in the rest of the magazines, try Promotional Marketing (www.promotionalmkt.com) 215-238-5300. OK, gotta go. Anybody seen a duck around here? Let's see, he was about a foot tall, and he kinda waddled...

BIG DISCOUNTS AND BETTER DIRECT RESPONSE IN... NEWSPAPER ADS

Surprisingly, there's not much buzz about direct response in newspaper space ads even in direct marketing inner circles. Yet ad placements continue to be profitable, and placements are on quite a grand scale. I guess no one likes to divulge all their secrets, especially when they're making big money at it.

With newspaper space ads, offers can be tested inexpensively, and successful venues and rollouts can be extremely profitable because the weekly circulation figures are surprisingly high. Run of press can reach well over 50 million readers. Each week.

Remnant Space

The first key to successful direct-selling newspaper advertising is buying cost-effectively, which means the first words in buying are "remnant space". Also called "standby," remnant space is the leftover blocks of space that remain unsold right before the newspaper's final page composition. Remnant space is also commonly found in magazine ad placements, where negotiated remnant rates can be as steeply discounted as 70% and 80% off list price.

Testing on a smaller geographic scale can be as simple as calling your local newspaper space sales rep and letting him or her know you're interested in remnant space. After receiving their short pitch on the value of buying space at the list price of open rate, feel free to request the rep call you back when some remnant space is available. Disconnect after letting them know you have an ad "ready to go" for immediate placement. They'll call back when the space is available - no one likes unsold space.

You can buy this type of individual ad placement with any of the thousands of papers nationwide. But what a pain in the neck: time consuming and lots of effort, and an incredible mess with individual newspapers billing you and individual checks to cut with each insertion.

When you purchase remnant space in bulk and your buys are national in scope, firms specializing in "remnant space ad distribution" make your life easier. They'll transmit your ads over the Internet to the various papers who accept remnant space purchase orders. When a newspaper has an opening, the publisher will strip in your ad in the last closing moments, right before the paper goes to press. The publishers are happy to do it even at the steeply discounted rate you'll be paying. Here's why...

Like two day old fish or a seat in an airplane when the door closes, ad space in newspapers is perishable. Once the paper heads towards the pressroom the ad space can no longer generate revenue and a house ad is used as a placeholder. As the unsold newspaper space heads for these final unprofitable moments, the publishers take what they can get for the space, knowing if it goes unsold and the paper actually goes on press, they get nothing. At this point in time most offers, even heavily discounted offers, look good.

Standby space ads can be a good consistent buy throughout the year. Ads run at a cost of between 50% to 80% OFF list rates, and sometimes sell for even less, especially at low demand periods like late summer and pre- and post-Christmas (most direct selling ad offers are not gift oriented).

Standby space ads in newspapers may be placed through several national placement sources specializing in remnant space buys. Some available space goes to the highest bidder in an open auction of remnant space on the web (Mediabids.

com), but most space is sold by firms dedicated to just reselling standby space.

"There is ALWAYS space available somewhere - and usually a good bit of it," says John Bosacker of Novus Print Media (763-458-5985, www.novusprintmedia.com), one of the larger distributors of "Standby" or "Remnant Space" ads. "At one time or another all newspapers face the problem of additional white space left over at the last minute... from stories that are cut or not quite ready at press time. We get first shot at that space."

In addition, advertisers pulling out at the last minute and last second glitches in production not only make room for on-hand ads, but make printers and composition editors drink heavily - and if they're good, die young. Ask Billy Joel.

Remnant space ads are purchased for clients in blocks of selected circulations, loosely outlined by either geographic boundaries or by selected individual newspapers. Further demographic may be targeted by runs in urban, suburban, or rural papers; and larger daily papers may be segregated out from smaller weeklies.

Besides newspaper, most magazines offer remnant prices at one point or another. Novus is also one of the nations largest magazine remnant space resellers. "You'd be surprised at some of the famous, huge national magazines offering 50%, 60%, 70% off their list rates," says Bosacker. He gave me some names but asked that I not publish them. "I don't think these magazines would like their names associated with discounted ad prices." John's pretty good about his confidential relationships, even though I inquired several different times.

Black and white ads - just like the predominance of the ads you saw when you were a kid - are still effective in this media. While most - if not all - magazines are now printed in full color, newspapers still remain primarily a black and white vehicle. This works to the advantage of the direct marketer:

ad composition can be less costly, but don't hold back on the creativity.

Testing different demographics is easy - and a key factor

Media buys can be national in scope, but you can also buy newspaper remnant space across a platform of specific smaller demographics. For example, you can specify that you'd like a million circulation in LA Times, in the hopes your offer will work for a strong urban demographic. Or, you can test a dozen smaller papers from urban to suburban to rural to see which ones elicit the highest response to your offer. You can purchase space in selected states or "test cities" that are known to be more responsive to new products and offers, or combine ad placement with product testing and price testing, or launches in retail stores. Additionally, advertisers generally get a good choice of geographic markets.

Initial testing should be broad, with tight tracking of both calls per thousand dollars spent, and calls per thousand circulation reached. The closing ratio for these figures will offer insight as to which types of demographic works best for your offer.

Sometimes specific newspaper sections may be purchased such as the movie pages or the business section. Since it's remnant space, there are no guarantees that your ad will be running in a particular paper or section or on a particular date. There is usually a two or three week window given to newspapers to feature your ad. At the end of this period, if the ad doesn't run the contract is canceled.

Both the distribution bureaus and the newspapers try to accommodate their advertisers. As with any advertising medium, all the players would like the ad to be successful: if the ad is successful and the marketer make money, the space distributor and the newspaper enjoy the revenue from the advertiser's longer insertion schedules.

When the ad runs and a response is generated, advertisers get a printout of names of papers where the ad appeared, usually referencing the section where the ad was run, along with the newspaper's circulation. These figures are used for tracking, and can be paired with the call center reports to see how the ad is pulling.

Reports then identify more profitable market segments, and ROI analysis. When all the figures are in from the initial placement testing, back-end analysis is performed: it's either an autopsy or the marketers figure out a more focused comprehensive plan to direct further placement of ads. Successful ads, as well as being placed in large circulations of papers, may run for years. I've personally seen small ads grow from tiny circulations in papers here and there to huge press runs of over 50 million, each week.

Graphics

Ads are required to be composed in two sizes, 10-1/2" x 6-7/8" and 10-1/2" x 5-11/16ths inch, the different sizes being necessary to accommodate both the standard and the slightly different tabloid newspaper format. Ads must be created in the specific page makeup software of the firm that is electronically distributing the ads, which means the ads need to be in Quark for Novus distribution. When the newspapers have an open space, the ad is transmitted to them electronically, imposed into their layout, and goes on press.

Key Elements

Most ads are soft offers: no price is given in the ad for the product, and the reader is directed to a toll free number for information or to order. As in most direct response, this is the objective of the ad: to generate a phone call. Different toll free numbers are assigned to different parameters of the ad placements, and the numbers are all tied to a call center, who receives the calls and does the selling, upselling and the tracking. Since no price is stated in the ad (soft offer), price testing can be done on the fly from the call center, and adjusted during the campaign according to the price resistance or ROI figures.

While price testing in real time is a great marketing option, better offers in print help drive calls. "Buy one, get one FREE!", "Buy two, get one FREE!", are very common, but the real copy that drives the phone to ring is "RISK-FREE OFFER!" and my personal favorite, "FREE TRIAL OFFER!". It's not really a free trial in the sense that we ship product and the consumer tries it... it's a free trial "offer": we sell the product and allow the consumer to try it free. They actually purchase it, with the option to return it for a full refund if they don't like it.

Once a prospect reaches the call center, the objective is to close the sale on the spot and offer the caller a quick upsell or two. The average call time is surprisingly low - averaging about seven minutes in duration. It's surprising to me that consumers make a buying decision that rapidly, it takes me that long to pick out which Q-Tips I'm buying at the supermarket. Heck, it takes me half an hour to select which jeans I'm wearing that day - and I work with just one person and usually don't go out of the office. If I have to go out for a business lunch, whoa, shirt selection takes... well, I get up early.

A good campaign can yield a range from a low of 45 to a high of 85 calls per thousand dollars spent. I've seen closure rates as high as 20%, but this isn't the way to bet. While some products lose money on the initial sale, re-ups, auto-ship and continuity sales for some items such as magazines, vitamin programs and nutraceuticals produce profits over the medium to long run. I believe placing people on auto ship is the highest art form in the direct marketer's business.

Products in all price ranges over $30 may work, the lower the price range the riskier - as media costs can eat up a good portion of the revenues. Offers of $75 to $150 may work well and the newspapers and placement bureaus find recurring ad revenues in long running nutraceuticals and vitamins ads.

Lately, much scrutiny has evolved from the FTC over the implied merchant ability and wording of ads for supplements and nutraceuticals. Unlike direct mail which targets selected recipients and avoids the eyes of the mass public and their accompanying government watchdogs, newspapers are a mass media and can't be shielded from federal eyes... and federal audit. You don't want to mess with the FTC or the FDA. They have deep pockets and don't care how much money you spend defending yourself from a suit - whether real or malicious. Ask Joe Sugarman.

Compliance

Compliance is a really big issue in nutraceutical and vitamin marketing. Both wording and claims must be selected with great care. Here's the bottom line: unless you're a drug manufacturer, you can't really say you can cure anything. And you can't imply it either. Did I mention you can't mention a disease because somehow to the FDA that implies you can cure it. I guess the bottom line is you can't do anything that may hurt pharmaceutical sales: the drug companies not only have all the money to keep you out of their business, it seems they own a good piece of the government as well. Who said money can't buy everything?

Nor can you say "eliminates pain," because you can't say "pain;" somehow in the eyes of some governmental agencies the word pain implies disease. So, while your copywriter is thinking, "At last a cure for Arthritis!" as your headline, your compliance attorney may be thinking "Soothes aching joints and muscles." You can't say, "Stops the Pain of Arthritis" or even "Eases the Pain of Arthritis!" You can say: "New for Arthritis Sufferers!" Just kidding - you can't say that, either. And no matter what you're selling, you can't say, "Stops Pain!" Well, you can say it, but just until you get caught. Compliance. Tough, huh?

You can say, "Aids in Joint Discomfort!" which makes it tough to sell product - even to someone who has severe joint pain. In reality, where I virtually think we are, if each ad was in 100% compliance it wouldn't say anything about anything... and very little would get sold.

So generally for the ads our firm creates we ask the client how much risk he's willing to accept. If they are loose, we aim for 70% to 80% compliance and hold our breath hoping we stay under the radar for a while. It may take several years till the client gets a letter from the FTC warning us to stop running the ad, their usual first step with an out-of-compliance ad. They'll then tell you the specific wording that is out of compliance. (You can see some of these letters on the web at the FTC site.)

If our client is scared, we aim for 85% compliance, and if they are really scared, we try to achieve 90% to 95% compliance, which is as close as anyone can get. No nutraceutical or vitamin ad is 100% risk free, no matter what anyone tells you.

If it's a long running campaign, from a client with deep pockets, we send the ad to the FTC and ask for a ruling. Of course, if they say it's out of compliance, you can't run it as it stands or you may face the certain consequences as soon as they find it's in the papers. This, of course, may take months... or years. But when they find it, it'll be like a slap in the face - and they are the original 900,000 lb gorilla.

Ad composition

All ads need a large, electrifying or benefit-heavy headline due to the skimming nature of the reader. The headline can make or break an ad in this particular media more than any other media. To be effective, use the Jeff Dobkin "Hundred to One Rule" when writing headlines - write 100, go back and pick out your best one. Hey, I didn't say you'd like it, I just said "to be effective...".

With the larger space of ads, a photo or graphic - more than one if copy permits - are a necessity. Placing a graphic or two in the ad visually attracts the reader's attention and stops the quick-skimming, page-flipping, short attention-spanned audience.

Attractive visuals give readers a graphic hook to remember, and provide some additional credibility and a visual point of reference to draw in readers and focus their attention. Photo captions are usually the highest read part of the ad, so a reader benefit should be mentioned here. No need to say "Here is the product," readers can see that. "Call now to see how much better you'll feel in just 21 days." will make the phone ring - thereby fulfilling the objective of the ad. In the end, all lines of copy should be measured against how well they work to fulfill the objective of the ad, which is "to call."

Most ads, being taller than wide, benefit from both a photo at the top and an additional photo or graphic near the bottom. Generally the bottom photo is of the product. This gives readers a reference of what they will receive when they order, building confidence that the product is real - since they can't feel or touch the product as in a retail store. An extra large phone number assures readers they can call. The phone number should be large enough to see when the paper is laying open to that page on a desk. Don't let the reader guess what he or she is to do.

To break up the type and keep the ad even more visually interesting, I usually like to include a graph or a chart. This mix of both copy and graphics boosts readership. Almost any kind of graph or chart will do, as it becomes part of the visual hook. With a little forward thinking, almost any kind of information can be displayed in graphic format.

Large Benefit-Oriented Subheads

While the visual layout and a distinctive graphic attracts readers, it's the copy that makes them call. Eyeflow starts at the top as the reader sees the graphic and reads the headline, glances past the smaller text to the bottom product shot and phone number. If interested at all, the reader goes back up to read the initial subhead and continues skimming the subheads if they are promising. If a subhead is particularly captivating, he reads the text block following it. If the whole thing is intriguing, he starts at the top text block and reads the ad until he loses interest or finishes.

There is usually room for two, three, or four subheads depending on the layout, and again each of these favor the "100 to 1 Rule". A short, crisp supporting paragraph or two follows each subhead, with the beginning line of each paragraph highly focused on keeping the reader in the copy.

As the paragraph ages and races towards the close, the copy changes from selling the product by offering the reader benefits to pointing the reader to "Pick up the phone and CALL NOW". Towards the end of each paragraph the words "Call Now" can usually be placed successfully: always remember, if the reader doesn't call, the ad fails. Never let the reader guess what he or she is supposed to do during or after reading the ad.

If the reader makes it to the end of the third paragraph, my guess is that the reader has quite a bit of interest and has pretty much made the commitment to read the rest of the ad, and I turn up the selling proposition and lay on heavy reader benefits and ask for the call several times.

Towards the end of the ad, once again the interested reader needs to be briefly reminded of the major benefits, and to be assured he is making the right decision to call as he receives a progressively harder "sell" to generate a phone call. It's "make it or break it" time in the ad and all stops are pulled out to make the phone ring. Readers at this depth of the ad are looking for concrete reasons to call, and for those that have decided to pick up the phone, they are looking for decision support and reinforcement that they have made the right decision, to call.

If you need an additional - but independent - selling space, place the bottom two or three lines of copy in a black box at the bottom of the ad and reverse out the letters. Make sure they are in bold so they don't fill in - newspapers usually have a 5 to 10% dot gain on press. This reversed out horizontal bar at the bottom additionally separates the ad visually from other ads on the page and gives the ad additional visual weight at the bottom, making it more distinct and increasing the separation from the ad below it.

A 2 point rule as a border around the ad separates it and sets it off from the rest of the ads and editorial on the page. Place any necessary disclaimers in tiny 5 or 6 point type at the very bottom of the ad. I usually bury a selling line or two in the disclaimer just in case anyone reads it. If the ad is service-oriented or sells merchandise in an old fashioned craftsmanship style, a scotch rule (thick then thin lines) around the ad is very handsome.

29 POINTS TO CREATING AN EFFECTIVE PRESS RELEASE

A PRESS RELEASE IS A SHORT, CRISP ONE-PAGE DOCUMENT you send to a magazine or newspaper editor. If published, it appears as if the magazine or newspaper editorial staff has written it. Here are 29 points to help you create a great release, increase your chances of having it published - and of getting a better response from a more highly qualified prospect.

29. Use 1" to 1-1/2" space at the top of the page as a header. The header contains contact information and is not considered part of the body of the release - the part that you would like to appear when the press release is published.

28. In the header print "Press Release" in a large, bold typeface. Alternate wording can be "News Release," "For Immediate Release," (my personal favorite), "NEWS," and so on. As long as a busy editor can see it's a press release at first glance, it works.

27. In the header include contact information containing your name, company name, phone number, fax number, email and the date. I also usually put the name of the release (the industry and a one or two word description of the release), and a "T" or "C" indicating if it's a trade or consumer release. (If it's a trade press release we talk about "fast turnover and high profit margins;" if it's a consumer release we talk about "customer benefits, product features and availability.")

26. The header should include a "kill date," after which you no longer wish the date to run. This information usually

applies to events, the kill date being the day after the event date. If there is no kill date, state "No Kill Date."

25. If you need the release to coincide with other media, indicate a "Start Date." For example, if you are releasing information about a new product, and would like all your publicity to appear all at the same time, let each publisher know. Otherwise, you'll have newspapers - who publish releases within 2 weeks - let the cat out of the bag, when your magazine press releases won't appear for a month, but more likely three to six months later.

24. Create the strongest headline you can possibly imagine. Of all the time you put into your release, spend the most on your headline. Spend an hour or two just thinking up the one line that will 1. make the editor think it will be a good story for their readers, 2. make the publisher look good so they will be interested in publishing it in their magazine or newspaper, 3. make every reader who might buy your product or use your service put it on their "Must Read" list, and 4. if possible, make it unattractive to those who will not buy your product or service - so you will save on your literature costs and mailing expense.

Here are three formula and examples to help you create great headlines.

23. Use the Headline formula, "FREE Booklet offers Valuable Information!" For example, a moving company headline might say: "FREE Booklet offers tips on packing valuables when you move." This booklet is simply two pages folded in half to 8-1/2" x 5-1/2" and nested together. It's low in cost to print, and can even be made on a copier. Result: very high interest from their target market (people who are going to move), and no interest from people who are outside their target market and are not going to move. So the moving company sends the booklet with a nice letter to the inquirer, and saves literature costs because people who aren't really prospects don't inquire.

22. Use the headline formula, "New Product Offers Benefit, Benefit, Benefit!" For example, "New computer screams with blazing speed, has enough storage room for 5,225,000 pages, yet fits in the palm of your hand!" Or, "Awesome New Book Demonstrates How To Market Any Product - in Under 6 Months!" (It's for the book, *Successful, Low Cost Direct Marketing Methods!*, by Jeff Dobkin. Best darn marketing book I've ever read!)

21. Speaking of Jeff, use the Jeff Dobkin "100 to 1 Rule for creating the best headlines." As found in the article of the same name on page 113 of the book, *Uncommon Marketing Techniques:* write 100 headlines, go back and pick out your best one. Hey, I didn't say you'd like it, I just said it would help you create a strong headline. Well, now you don't have to buy the book, unless you want the excellent marketing tips and techniques - and bad jokes - that fill the other 269 pages.

20. Start your press release with the important elements first. Just like a newspaper story, press releases are created with a pyramid style of writing: the most important elements at the top. For example, a newspaper story may have the headline "Fire Kills 3;" the story starts, "three persons die, and seven more were injured in a 5 alarm..." and it goes on fact by fact in order of relevancy. Trailing at the story's end may be what the neighbors said or how many donuts the firemen ate while putting out the blaze. Editors know to cut from the bottom.

19. Don't use fluffy words or lots of adjectives. If it sounds like an ad, as opposed to sounding like a news story, it will be rejected by the editor, and consequently not selected for publication.

18. Start your body copy with one or two of your biggest benefits. This is an unusual style of release I originated and it's an anomaly to point 15. I call it the benefits-first release. Since editors traditionally cut information from the bottom, if you are smooth in sneaking in one or two benefits in the very first line of the release they usually won't be cut. Remember:

benefits - what's in it for the reader - are why people buy your product or call you with an inquiry.

17. Keep it to one page. You're not writing the new version of "War and Peace." Two-page press releases are much harder to get read let alone get placed. There are, however, "Feature Releases" - which are usually written for a specific magazine. If you think your storyline is worth a feature story, call the editor first (or write a query letter pitching the story proposal) to make sure you're not wasting your time writing a long press release that's going nowhere.

16. Use courier style type, 12 point, and double space your body copy. If it runs long - over a page, or you need more white space, go to 10 point. If you still need more room go to a more condensed face like Bookman, Century Schoolbook or Times Roman which are much more condensed typefaces. If you still need more space, take out a big red pen and cross out half of what you've written - it's too long.

15. Take out a big red pen and cross out half of what you've written anyhow. Edit severely. The closer you can come to "This press release contains no apparent bullshit, er... extraneous material," the more likely it is to be published.

14. Proof your work carefully. If your work is filled with typos, mistakes and poor grammar, the editor will think his or her readers will get poorly written literature (if anything at all) or a lousy product - either of which will reflect badly on his publication. Result: your press release won't run.

13. Include contact information in the body of the release. The last paragraph of your release should contain your or your company name, address, phone, fax and email. If your release is direct-selling and you hope to get any direct sales, the price must be included. If your price is really high, leave it out and ask readers to write or call for more information.

Remember, the story appears as if written by the magazine or newspaper - so write about your firm in the third person: "Contact them at..." "Their address and phone number is..."

12. End with ### to show it's the end. End newspaper re-leases with -30-.

11. Call the editor. For the top 5 or 10 placements you'd re-ally like to have your released published (more if you like to use the phone), call the editor FIRST and ask, "Are you the person I should send this press release to?" This sets up a "Can you help me?" relationship in under 30 seconds. If they say yes, give them your 30-second to 1-minute pitch, then send your release. If they say no, get the name of the person who receives releases, and start this exact same conversation all over again.

(Note: most editors are usually helpful, except around the closing date of the magazine at the end of the month - then they're usually cranky). Find out if they're "on deadline" before you ask for them.

10. If you get nervous after sending a release and in hindsight decide to call the editor, never - and I mean never - say "Did you get my release?" This makes editors angry: you'll be the 10,000th person who has asked them that very same ques-tion... this month. Instead, say "I'm calling to see if I can give you any additional information on our new..." and give your product. Then you can mention you sent a press release a week ago that's in a purple folder/envelope (so it'll be easy to find). If they like what you have to say, they'll let you know that they'll be happy to find your release, or I'm sure you'll be happy to send another one.

9. How to estimate the value of the release. When your press release is published, take the number of column inches of space your press release consumes in the magazine, then figure out what that space would have cost you if you bought it as ad spacc. Then add 25%, because the value of editorial is much greater than ad space, because of the greater cred-ibility as it appears as editorial.

8. Select your press release list with care. You can find the magazines, the newspapers and the editors' names in some excellent, easy-to use-directories and on-line resources. The

directories we use here in our offices are excellent choices: Bacon's Magazine Directory and Bacon's Newspaper Directory (800-621-0561), Burrelle's Media Directories which include Burrelle's Magazines and Newsletters, Burrelle's Daily Newspapers and Non-Daily Newspapers) (800-631-1160) (now Burrelles is known as Burrelles/Luce and is On-Line only); Oxbridge Communications Standard Periodical Directory, and the Oxbridge Directory of Newsletters (800-955-0231), and SRDS Publication Business Advertising Source and Newspaper Advertising Source (800-232-0772). These directories can also be found in most libraries, and now also online, where you can buy a subscription to the most up-to-the-minute editorial data.

7. Make an A and B list for each industry. The A list editors get a phone call before sending them your release. The B list editors simply get press releases with nice cover letters. For our press campaigns, we usually send 80 to 100 releases for a minor release, and up to 500 press packages for a major release. How many you send will all depend on the size of the industries or markets you are trying to reach.

6. Include a Photo. We usually send 5" x 7" black and white photos with every release - it adds a visual hook to the story and most of the time the photo gets printed. It also increases the perceived press release package value (nice release, nice photo = additional credibility for your firm).

5. Send press releases every few months. A single press release is not a campaign. Grooming the press and getting consistent publicity is a continual process.

4. Send a letter with every press release. If you called the editor as mentioned above, start your letter with "Thanks for receiving my call. It was a pleasure speaking with you," even if it wasn't. This reminds the editor that you were the one that called, how much the publication of this release means to you, and can increase the chance of your press release being published from 5% to 70%.

3. In the letter you send with your press release, don't say "Enclosed is a press release." They can see that. Produce a

letter that gives your firm and product additional credibility, and also gives a savvy editor additional copy points they can pick up and use in your publication write-up.

2. Remember the function of the press release is to sell products or generate phone calls. I have a client who bragged to me that his PR agency had gotten his firm a mention in The Wall Street Journal. "Did you get any calls?" I always ask. "Did you get a lot of business from it?" I continue before they can say "no."

Unless you simply want your ego stroked, a write-up is a waste of time if it doesn't generate a response. If you want your ego stroked, buy a dog - it's cheaper. If you want more business, write and correctly present a well constructed press release.

1. If your press released is published, don't forget to follow up with a nice "thank you" letter. You've received excellent value for your time and effort, and a thank you letter shows that you appreciate it.

The logical conclusion to a successful press campaign is the knowledge base of which magazines bring in results and sales for you - so that you can place ads in them. Place ads in the top drawing publications that published your release. While most people look at ads as an expense, we cherish magazines and papers that can deliver our focused message to a responsive, target audience - time after time, month after month - and bring us a profitable return. When we find a medium that's profitable for us, we run ads in it forever. We use press releases as a low-cost testing vehicle to find these profitable magazines.

DETERMINING
MARKET SIZE

WHEN TRYING TO FIGURE OUT MARKET SIZE the first place I check is the magazine directories such as Bacon's Magazine Directory, Burrelle's Media Directory, Oxbridge Communications Directory of Periodicals, and SRDS Magazine Media Source to name a few. You can find out in a few minutes just how many different magazines serve this market. The number of magazines is a good indication of size. Remember, the advertising revenue supports the magazines and the industry buyers support the advertisers.

Note how expensive the ad space is in the magazines. A good way to see the comparative figures for magazines is to look in Oxbridge Communications Magazine Directory - they give you a CPM or Cost Per Thousand for each magazine. This shows you the cost to reach a thousand people with a full page black and white ad in that magazine. It makes comparing magazine advertising costs much easier. Hummm... Thanks, Oxbridge!

Next check the circulation of each magazine: how large is their circulation? This is probably the single best method of assessing market size. There will be some pretty consistent figures showing how many copies are distributed to industry personnel. If you really want to see just where all those magazines are being sent, call the publisher and ask for a "Media kit." This free package is how the publishers themselves market their own magazines to advertisers. In the package will be a copy of an independent audit showing who qualifies to receive the magazine, how they are qualified, and shows the circulation breakdown of exactly where all the copies are sent.

There are usually some magazines that have 30% or 50% more circulation than most of the others. These periodicals

doesn't know anything about marketing!

may have more relaxed qualifications to receive their magazine. Their readership may be of lesser value because of this, but maybe not - depending on what you are selling, and how tightly focused your audience profile needs to be targeted. If you want to address an entire marketplace by sheer numbers, these larger circulation magazines may be the way to go.

While the larger distribution magazines may be more freely circulated, the smaller circulation magazines may be sent to a more tightly qualified subscriber list; or the magazines may be sent only to "Paid" subscribers - which really knocks down circulation. Paid circulation, however, may mean better readership, a higher quality, or a more focused publication.

Some paid magazines are sent strictly to association members, so be on the lookout for that, too. The magazine is paid for out of the members' dues. These publications may be good, or horrible, even though their subscriber list is large and it's shown as a paid-for magazine. The horrible magazines simply get thrown out by the subscriber. I throw out the AAA magazine that comes with AAA membership, but I'm sure their circulation figures include me as a reader. I suspect nobody reads it, as it's one of the worst magazines I've ever seen: filled with blatantly biased articles designed solely to sell their own products and the products hawked by paying advertisers in their magazine. Ugh. And I thought there was always supposed to be a dividing line between editorial and advertising.

Other ways to assess market size

While at the library looking over the magazine directories, head over to the reference desk and drag out the SRDS Directory of Mailing Lists (SRDS List Source) along with the Oxbridge Communications Directory of Mailing Lists. Look up the industry you are researching and find out how many lists serve it. Then note the size of each list in that market. This will give you a few more numbers to think about. While there, see if you can find out if the numbers are increasing or decreasing for that marketplace. That will give you an idea if the market is growing or declining.

Next, get the catalogs of some of the major list vendors. These vendors can be found in the direct marketing trade journals: you can get a free copy of each of these trade journals by calling the publishers and asking for a media kit, or a sample copy for advertising evaluation, the magazines will go right out via first class mail. The publishers' phone numbers of said direct marketing magazines can be found in... the magazine directories, thanks for asking. Call all the list vendors who have ads and ask if they have a catalog. I've already done this and have written up each catalog, size, page count, organization, information they provide and so forth. You can call me (610-642-1000) for a copy of my article "Free Catalogs of Mailing Lists." We'll talk about its cost when you call.

When you get the list catalogs, look up the industry you're researching. Here, you'll be able to see the statistics of how many businesses there are in this particular industry in the U.S. You'll also be able to find out business size by income or number of employees. In some instances you'll be able to get the names of individuals and their positions. If you're really savvy, you can get this information on the web, and then click-in some overlays to find out size (and wealth) related questions, like how many businesses are in each income range, how many have over 100 employees - or over 50 employees, or under 10 employees - or whatever marketing segment you're looking for. You can get breakouts by demographics, by geographics, zip codes, living clusters, or any which of 50 different ways - and you'll be able to find out this information in real time, er... sort of. Look up lists on the Internet. If you need immediate counts, this can be the fastest place to get them or at least the first round of them anyhow. There's nothing like calling the list vendor for real information and more articulated breakouts.

If you're researching consumer markets, or even industrial markets that are fairly large, you might check the catalog directories of Oxbridge Communications or Woodbine House. These will give you an idea of what is sent to that segment of the population. So if you're marketing a particular type of blue jeans, you'll know right away there are hundreds of apparel catalogs, and your market is indeed huge.

Finally, look in the reference books of associations - such as the Gale Encyclopedia of Associations, the Columbia House Book of Associations, and the Leadership Directory of Associations. The size of the association will give you an immediate industry assessment. But then, call the association for that industry - the folks at the association headquarters will be very knowledgeable about the market, its size, its strengths and weaknesses, the magazines and all the major players. You can probably also get a list of the major players - often the association directors - and call them for still further information. These heavyweights are usually exceptionally helpful - that's why they are directors of the associations in the first place.

To me, establishing market size isn't the amount of money spent in an industry. For example, to say the motorcycle industry is a 4 billion dollar industry doesn't tell me very much. This figure is meaningless to small businesses -- and it's especially harmful to say "This market does 4 billion a year, if we can just get a 1% share...." As far as I know, no marketing plan correctly takes the industry figure and figures a percentage of what they will receive in revenue. Of course I've only been in marketing for about 25 years. When I look at a market I need to know how easy or difficult it will be to introduce a product or service to that industry. So I need to see how entrenched my client's competition is, and how high the entrance barriers are, and...

Here's some of the other stuff I look at: is the industry product intensive? Are there tons of magazines? And do all the magazines continually show huge groups of new products? I know it will make my client's products harder to get noticed and thus harder to bring to market. Lots of magazines, lots of ads, make an industry very product intensive, and with our product we'd be just one of the pack. While it might make it very easy to get our first press release featured, subsequent releases will be difficult to place.

Are there huge competitors in direct competition with our own products? If there are, they may have all the major distributors tied up distributing their products, so they won't be able to distribute ours. Additionally, we may need to address their strengths in our marketing plan and stay away from those areas -- or figure out their weaknesses and attack them. We may also need to adjust our price or our warranties to align with theirs.

If it looks like we can attack the industry with a reasonable budget, if we can find and reach the major players and alert them of our products and services, if we can test the media with press releases before committing to an ad schedule, if there aren't hundreds of people marketing the same product - or something close enough that our product can't be realistically differentiated from the pack, if the competition isn't big enough to cut their price in half so that we must meet their discounted pricing (allowing us no profit) hey - I say we take a shot.

THE SIMPLE OBJECTIVE OF A MARKETING CAMPAIGN

THE FUNCTION OF MARKETING is to present goods and services to people who need or want them, and entice them to buy. This includes alerting people that your product is available, showing prospects its features and benefits, and making them an offer they won't want to refuse.

In a broad sense, marketing is one of the three phases of any business, the other two being operations and finance. Sales is a part of the marketing arm, as is advertising. Advertising is knowing what to say, marketing is knowing where to say it. Sales is not marketing. The sales manager does not become the vice-president of marketing, he becomes the vice-president of sales.

A part of marketing is determining the industry entrance barriers, investigating the industry pricing strategies and setting prices. It's also examining the media and its costs and relative effectiveness. Marketing is also finding and analyzing the competition, discovering the scope and depth of the number of people who wish to buy your goods, the saturation level of people who already own it, and the maturity of how long your product has been around. Marketing includes the function of the selection of additional products to sell, along with the selection of distribution channels in which to sell them. All the while the marketing department is keeping an eye on making a profit.

Most importantly it's the marketer's job to satisfy customers enough for them to purchase, then to come back and purchase again; and finally to earn the privilege and the trust of having customers refer other customers and their friends. If your customers don't come back, or you don't get good referrals, your product - or your marketing - stinks. This one fact separates the good marketeers from the great marketeers. Getting repeat business and getting referrals are two of the lowest cost, most effective ways to market both goods and services.

The objective of a marketing campaign is to correctly identify the individuals or groups of people who are the most likely to purchase your goods or services - so you can promote your brands to them. The better you are able to define your best potential customers, and separate them from everyone else, the more effective your marketing campaign.

Let me put it this way: the better you are at defining your target group, the more effective you will be at reaching them. Consequently, you'll waste less money on the expense of advertising - and trying to sell to people who aren't interested in purchasing your goods and services. Thus, the better your marketing, the lower your marketing costs.

This "market research" phase of investigative marketing is where we separate the "not interested" and the "can't afford it" along with the "not quite ready" and the "unsure" and cast them into one group called "expense". Then we take the "we'd like to purchase" group and put them in a holding pattern, dousing them with constant reminders of our brand, our offer and good will and keep them close at hand, while we actively turn our immediate attention to the "We're ready to buy, here's our money!" group. Then we sell the last group something, as our first priority. Cash flow is the first name of any good marketing campaign.

But the party's not over, yet. If the campaign is a good one, the marketing plan should focus on the best places to find more - clones - of these "most likely to purchase," folks and the "We're ready to buy, here's our money!" groups and assess how they can be reached most effectively (i.e.: at the least cost.)

For example, if I was introducing a new product and found that the local sheet metal workers here in Philadelphia were purchasing it in good quantity, the first place I'd look for more of the same would be in the magazines that serve the sheet metal industry. "Sheet Metal Working Today," and "Modern Sheet Metal Times" magazines would make my job a lot easier, faster and cheaper.

If the market is fragmented, individual buyers may be scattered across the country, or across many industries, without a way to reach them as a group through a selected set of magazines, trade shows or other mass-media avenues. In this case, perhaps they can be defined by a SIC code, or targeted and reached through a direct mail list. Thus they can be reached individually at their doorstep through a mailing. Now we look for the most focused and targeted mailing lists, custom designed and further enhanced to the specific defined criteria of our target group.

It is through the medium of direct mail that we can really tighten the selection criteria parameters that defines our best and most focused target niche from the entire marketing universe. So if we were looking for people with diabetes we might be able to reach them through "Diabetes Today" magazine. But if we were looking for people with Type II Diabetes in their early stages, we might be able to find a mailing list of people with Diabetes with an overlay for "Type II" and an additional selection overlay of "early stage." Depending on our product usage parameters we may wish to select even more overlays such as gender, or if our products were expensive, income.

Direct mail, when executed correctly, can be used with the precision of a surgeons knife to extract perfect prospect models from the masses, who often range from the pick of the litter to the vague and disinterested. Direct mail is an example of one of the hundreds of ways to get the message out to viable prospects-and if selected carelessly, others.

It's the marketing department of a company that selects the medium in which to contact and acquire customers. Common ways of mass media advertising include TV, radio and newspapers - which are used mainly for consumer offers because of their broad reach across many industries, age groups, income levels and types of positions. A great advantage of newspapers is their high density geographic base of coverage.

Magazines - one of my favorite ways to dredge for marketing data as well as to place advertising - may be used for both trade and consumer products. Industrial magazines, and specialty consumer magazines have a unique ability to penetrate a specific industry or market niche with broad reach, albeit little depth. For example, there are about 50 publications that are sent to the motorcycle industry, about half are trade magazines going to dealers, accessory shops, manufacturers and so forth.

Computer geeks, who often don't get enough satisfaction from just owning a computer, generally love to get whipped into a purchasing frenzy to buy yet the next and latest model by the computer trade magazines. I say that because there are over 450 different magazines that are sent - each and every month - to the range of computer industry personnel. Too bad about their new machine: as it touched their desk for the very first time it was already obsolete.

Trade shows are usually industry specific, and tend to be industrial in nature, although a few big shows span several industries. That not-with-standing, consumer marketing through shows is prevalent in a core of industries. Who hasn't heard of the Auto Show, the Boat Show or the Home Show. There are over 10,000 trade shows staged around the U.S. each year. These are great for face to face information gathering, selling and lead generation. I've never been to a trade show I didn't like, or didn't learn something from.

Let's not forget, ugh, telemarketing; while I don't like getting unsolicited calls - there are types of campaigns for which telemarketing is very effective. The telephone is an effective instrument and sales tool - generally much better than a sheet of paper sent in an envelope. But, telephone calls are more labor intensive - er, expensive, too. While I can mail 5,000 pieces of mail in a few days right from my office, I'd be hard pressed to have more than 20 to 30 calls an hour from each staff member. One commonality amongst our staff: we all hate the phone. Some people are good at it, though.

And of course there's nothing like a personal sales call from your staff, or rep firms that are common to most industries. As if the previous wasn't enough, now we have to suffer through fields of email, affiliate marketing and storms of continually popping-up banner ads on the Internet. By the way, if you're e-mailing me, I assure you I didn't opt-in for ANY email program, no matter what anyone told you. While there's a good bit of shake out, the Internet really has changed the face of marketing.

It is the people in the marketing department who decide which features and benefits turn-on the people in each distinct market niche. Their interpretation of data from research, their experience, or sometimes plain old seat-of-the-pants judgment leads the department heads to judge how best to approach each group of prospects to make them respond. The marketing department also selects what the offer is, what size ad should be placed and most importantly... what to have for lunch. Just kidding. I meant, most importantly in which magazines to place ads. They also select which mailing lists to rent, the criteria to judge and rate each list, and how many different lists to test.

In most firms the marketing department directs the PR department, determines which magazines and newspapers we should send press releases for publication; and in fact, the structure, nature, scope and depth of the press releases campaign.

The company marketing gurus decide how to construct the press release campaign to get the most response, and whether to cast a tight net to get more qualified prospects, or a loose net to get more less-qualified suspects. Then the department devises the offer and what the respondent gets - whether it's a free sample, call for information, write for information, bingo card response (ugh), stop in store, buy one get one free or any of a myriad of ways to make the potential customer speak out in some way to let us know he may be interested in our products or services. The customer speaks by alerting us of his interest so that we may give him further and more detailed information in an effort to induce him to buy. Or the customer can actually cast his or her vote on our marketing correctness by purchasing the product.

The marketing function also includes setting price through the use of various pricing considerations. There are hundreds of ways to set prices, and thousands of formulae - of which only a short handful are correct. I personally feel the price should be high enough to generate a profit, add some cushioning for growth, and still allow the sale of your products in a competitive marketplace. In direct marketing it is the market that sets the correct price - and testing will reveal the best sales level at the most profit.

Price consideration is determined by 1. if the market is price sensitive or need driven 2. how long the order processing cycle is 3. how long till we can deliver 4. the repeat buying cycle 5. how often the customer will purchase 6. what it costs to reach each customer (CPM) 7. the customer acquisition cost 7. the cost of each inquiry (CPI) 9. the cost of each sale (CPO- cost per order) and finally, 10. the lifetime value of a customer. I like to to find out if customers can get comparable products anywhere else, what is our perceived image of quality, who is the a price leader and are they vulnerable to a price attack, and if we can we leverage our market position to a price advantage.

Keep in mind that the cost of marketing additional products goes down considerably from the costs associated with your original sale. In fact, if you market other products, your marketing costs may at times be close to zero. Most often, your very best prospect for buying additional products is someone who has just purchased from you, especially if they are happy with your original products and services. They are my most favorite marketing target group as they are usually the most likely to immediately purchase again from us.

So marketing, then, is a system to deliver your message to the maximum number of interested people, to produce the maximum number of sales at the lowest possible cost and at the highest amount of fair profit. Then, the function of marketing is to sell the purchaser something else or establish him as a repeat buyer by making sure he is a satisfied customer. Hummm, perhaps all the rest is bullshit?

THE 2-MINUTE INTERVIEW

DALE KING HERE. Today, I'm interviewing World Famous Author and Entrepreneur, Jeffrey Dobkin. Hello Jeffrey, how are you?

Jeffrey Dobkin: Wow, Dale... I'm much better now that I'm "World Famous". It's funny, I don't think of my fame at all. I know my articles have been in and out of a few hundred magazines, but I'm always surprised when someone notices who the heck wrote the article and figures out it was me. So, this is fame... sitting here at a computer typing 8 hours a day?

Dale King: Jeffrey, tell our readers how and when you got started marketing on the Internet.

Jeffrey Dobkin: Let's see, what time is it? Just kidding. The Internet? OHMYGOD! Is that still around? I'm pretty recent to the Internet. 25 years in direct marketing, and I've just been visiting porno sites on the Internet for... Oh, I mean "marketing" on the Internet for... well I'm just now starting.

Dale King: Some Internet marketing experts advise newbies to steer clear of Internet marketing, because it's too competitive. Do you agree with that assessment?

Jeffrey Dobkin: Yes, and stay out of print advertising, because that's too competitive, too. And don't take booth space out at trade shows, either. Or TV ads.

It's all competitive. The toughest part about marketing on the Internet is getting people to your site. Then, running a close second: I've seen more orders and clients lost because of a poorly designed site.

My first preference for any off-line advertising is to get people to CALL on the PHONE, and not to go to a website. My first preference for any online advertising is to get people to CALL on the PHONE, also.

That way we can track the ad response, track the placement vehicle (the magazine or paper the ad was placed in), and see exactly what a person wants or needs. If you send a respondent of an ad to a website and he or she leaves the site without ordering, you don't really know why, do you?

Was it that he or she didn't like your product? Your services? Or your site design was bad, or poor navigation, or he timed out, or perhaps his wife just came in when he was going to order and told him she knew he was sleeping with the cute little red haired girl that worked in the 7-11 because she found a large Slurpee cup in his sock drawer wrapped in a pair of women's underwear and she knew he would never get a large Slurpee because he was too cheap. And then she didn't believe you when you said the underwear was yours. Or, did that just happen to me?

Dale King: Is that your final answer?

Jeffrey Dobkin: Well, you get the idea. Whether it's an ad or a website you send clients to, most of the time I still like to generate a phone call. I guess I'm just old school. Can you sell from a website? Sure. But unless the person is bound and determined to order, it can be a tough sell, just like selling from a brochure you send. It can be done, but it's easier to sell a phone call than sell a product from a sheet of paper. If I can make the reader call - I can then sell the product myself. So, I still like driving orders to the phone.

Dale King: How is Internet marketing different now, as opposed to when you first got started online?

Jeffrey Dobkin: Well, last Wednesday when I got started it was much earlier in the week. Now it's Friday and the difference is now that it's Friday, I go home early. Oh, wait... I go home early on Wednesday, too. I play racquetball at 4:00 PM and I never miss a game unless it's to take my kids to baseball or somewhere.

Difficulties marketing on the Internet are similar to when I started: can't drive people to your site, can't get to the top of the search engines, online selling is still rough because good order pages are expensive.

Dale King: How important has goal-setting been to your overall success?

Jeffrey Dobkin: I haven't set any goals other than get famous, and here I am working on my computer 8 hours a day so I guess that ain't happening yet.

Actually, most days I work under different parameters. My only real goal is to save lives by the lifesaving technique I've discovered. Readers can read about it at my website, www.dobkin.com. It's in the "Members Only" section - which is really an open section. It's entitled "A Technique to Delay Brain Death in Heart Attack Victims" but the procedure also works in drownings victims, drug overdose, suffocation, electrocution victims and some others. So... if you're reading this - please fast forward to my website and read that. It may save your life or the life of someone close to you. You can learn the technique in under one minute and it works instantly in time of crisis.

Now, back to reality - where I virtually think we are. My daily routine is to write articles which I enjoy doing, write client material like direct marketing letters, newspaper ads, magazine ads, or write marketing plans, which I also enjoy; and finish my books which seem to take forever because I'm so long-winded. My primary title, How To Market A Product for Under $500 weighs 2-1/2 lbs. I stopped writing so people would be able to pick it up. I have about a dozen copies left so if you want one ($29.95) call now. When these sell out it will only be available in PDF format and also as a POD title - for $75.

So as you can see, goal setting isn't my first priority. OOOPS. Can I take all that back? No... guess not. That's what you get when you call so early. Or late. Or whenever. Or, did you just send me these questions in an email?

Dale King: How important has reading been to your overall success?

Jeffrey Dobkin: I read a lot. Not many books, but I skim and read over 125 magazines a month. To keep up with trends, to keep up with the industries my clients serve, and to make sure my articles get good placement. Even though I'm in a lot of magazines, it's still thrilling to open one up and see an article of mine has made it into print. I know editors have a huge selection to pick from, so I know it's a privilege to have mine placed.

Dale King: If you could recommend one book that all Internet marketers should read, what would it be?

Jeffrey Dobkin: It would be my book, How To Market A Product for Under $500 (Or Uncommon Marketing Techniques) because I need the sales. Actually, you don't have to buy my books, just send me the money. Kidding. OK, no I wasn't. They're great books for Internet marketing because they are completely filled with practical tips and techniques in direct marketing - which is what the Internet is all about - direct marketing and direct sales. Not much technical Internet stuff - I leave that to the, you know, geeks. Oh... sorry Dale...

Dale King: In your opinion, what technology has changed Internet marketing the most over the last 5 years?

Jeffrey Dobkin: The Internet in itself is relatively young since Al Gore started it a few years back. Well, that's what he said, and politicians don't lie, do they? The Internet has been advancing in leaps and bounds since its inception, and is still relatively young. Just wait a couple of years, and streaming video will take over. That's my belief.

The most progressive technical changes are the greater availability of faster connections. Software enhancements are certainly upfront too as the search engines and search options and pay-for-search have come about. Which is not only a big business, but a great technical option for advertisers. SEs are the most wonderful gift to humanity, and especially great for us marketers.

Personalization software to support marketing and mass marketing is becoming better. You can now write a effective letter and send it to a list of subscribers and make them think they are the only ones receiving it, or one of a very few.

I'm not talking about stripping a guy's name and address into the letter like in cheap direct mail solicitation ads - and saying "Since you, Jeffrey Dobkin, who lives in Bala Cynwyd Pennsylvania." I'm talking about having the customer give you information then sorting it for relevancy and sending only information the customer wants.

For example, American Airlines asks its Skymiles participants what places they'd like to travel to, then when special prices come up for those destinations they send members an email with just those places - all other destination emails are suppressed. The client sees only relevant information - he's happy. And your open rate hits close to 100%. That's database marketing at its best. And it's getting better.

Dale King: What new technology do you see changing Internet marketing over the next 5 years?

Jeffrey Dobkin: Video feeds, and the technology filtering down to give everyone the knowledge to easily make videos. It's almost here now. The big drawback is I can flip though a magazine and read the parts that are relevant to me and be outta there in 10 minutes. But with video you have to watch the whole thing in real time. So if the good part in a magazine is on page 125, I can go right there. If the good part in a video is at minute 140, I'll be long gone.

Search will keep redefining itself, getting better - as long as Google doesn't sell out - and continue to be a real blessing to everyone. And marketing will get more serious and easier for smaller players. Most businesses will have a web presence, and it will be more necessary, and easier to create.

Dale King: What person has influenced you the most in your lifetime, and how?

Jeffrey Dobkin: My older brother has been very supportive of my personal life. He's freed me from having to pay a huge mortgage that was crushing me financially for a few years. Without that, I wouldn't have been able to take the time or have the creative freedom to write the books and articles I enjoy writing. Without his help, I'd be too busy serving clients, which pays the bills but doesn't afford me the opportunity to help others as I do through my books and articles.

Dale King: If you could give my readers one piece of advice, what would it be?

Jeffrey Dobkin: Buy my books. Seriously. If your readers need thousands of inside tips on marketing and direct marketing - my books really are a Godsend. Here's why: Over the past 25 years I've gone into thousands of businesses and asked what works, what doesn't? I wrote down all the techniques that worked well for almost everyone. So, in a sense my books took 25 years to write. Hummm.... seems like it, anyhow.

Your readers can go to my website and read some of the articles to see my style and information-rich content. These are the books I needed when I was a young man learning about business. I stayed up many nights looking for this information.

Dale King: Thank you very much Jeffrey. I appreciate you taking the time to do this interview.

Dale King is a good guy and can be found lurking around his website, guruknowledge.org, where he has published many excellent business articles including some of my my own writing. Hope he fixed all those typos...

14 MORE QUESTIONS IN MARKETING

Here are 14 more questions I'm often asked about the different phases of marketing. Starting with direct mail - getting your package opened:

Direct Mail

Q. What does it cost to mail 1,000 to 5,000 pieces of mail.

A. Unless you're in the direct mail business and mail all the time, figure the costs between 45 cents and 55 cents per envelope. This includes postage, envelope, letter, and brochure.

Here's a bonus: If you assign 50¢ for each piece mailed it's easy to figure the mathematics to break even. A 10,000 piece mailing will cost you $5,000. How many orders do you need to receive to cover this cost? And what percent response is that? If you make $50 profit on each order, you need 100 orders (100 x $50 = $5,000) to break even on 10,000 piece mailing. That's a 1% response rate. Achievable, but difficult. So...

Q. What's a good response to a mailing?

A. Anything that makes money. If you're selling a 12 million dollar airplane and get one inquiry from your 100,000 piece mailing - and he buys a plane, you were successful. But I usually figure 1/2 to 1% as pretty good, and try to calculate if my clients will show a profit at one half of one percent.

So the real question is "Will you be profitable if one person out of 200 buys? Or, if one out of 100 buys?" You have to work out your numbers from the back end first, to see what conversion ratio you need to break even or - heaven forbid - make money.

That's why products selling for $15 or $20 bucks aren't successful - you need too high a percentage response to make money in direct mail. At a cost of $500 per thousand pieces mailed, with a 1% response - or 10 calls - you need to sell enough to cover a $500 cost, or $50/order after product and processing costs - just to break even.

Q. Should you use teaser copy on your envelope or not?

A. Yes, and no. A great teaser line - if it's clever - will overcome a bulk mail stamp (now called standard mail) and can drive the recipient to open the envelope.

On the other hand, if you want more a of a professional look, and don't want to use a teaser line, the next best way to get recipients to open your letter: design it to look like it's a personal letter - put a live, first class stamp on it and hand write or ink-jet the address. Then use your name (with no company name) and your business address in the upper left hand corner. Now it looks like a personal letter, and most everybody will open it. It's important to have the recipient's address imaged directly on the envelope - no label.

Q. What's the best way to come up with great teaser copy for your envelope?

A. It's the Jeff Dobkin 100 to 1 Rule: Write 100 lines, go back and pick out your best one. Yep. This technique, as first reported in my book, Uncommon Marketing Techniques, also works to create a headline for an ad or a press release; or the first line of your letter or the body copy of an ad. I didn't say you'd like it, I just said it works.

Q. OK, Dobkin - what's your own best teaser copy to get an envelope opened?

A. My favorite teaser copy for envelopes is "Gift Certificate Enclosed!" Everyone will open because... if only to see what it is. Also - they're 1. cheap to print and 2. light to ship (on only 1/3 or 1/4 of a sheet of paper), 3. have no cost at all until redemption, 4. can be directed at high margin or excess merchandise, and are 5. naturally easy to track. Any arguments?

Copywriting

Q. What's your best trick for writing when you can't seem to come up with anything good?

A. Start anywhere, then go back and cross out your first sentence. Having a really bad day? Go back and cross out your first paragraph. This will pull you right into the heart of your copy.

Q. Give two of your favorite headline formula

A. New Product Offers Benefit, Benefit, Benefit (New lightweight tennis racquet is faster to swing, easier to control and hits harder); and Free Booklet Offers Valuable Information; for example: Call for Free Booklet "How to Pack China for Moving!" The strength of the booklet title determines the response.

Marketing Questions

Q. What is the objective of the "marketing function"?

A. To narrow the prospect list to "only the people who are the very most likely to purchase, when they are ready to purchase" and delete everyone else.

Q. How do you find all the magazines that go to any industry?

A. There are excellent magazine directories at the library. You can find any industry and the magazines that serve that industry in under 5 minutes. The best directories are Bacon's Magazine Directory, Oxbridge Communication's Directory of Periodicals, and the SRDS Directory of Magazines.

Q. How can I get a sample copy of any magazine to see if it has a good profile audience for me to market to?

A. As a potential advertiser, call the publisher and ask for a "Media kit." Sample copies will be sent along with advertising rate information by first class mail. Their response will be very prompt. Be sure to ask for any annual directory issue at that time, too. Directory issues are usually only available once a year when they come out - unless you request them with a media kit. Nice trick, huh? My publisher friends are gonna' hate me for this one.

Q. Where can I buy a mailing list?

A. Sources for lists include: List brokers (these can be found in the phone book), List compilers as found in the direct marketing trade journals, magazine publishers (who usually sell their lists), associations, on the web, catalog publishers; also check out the SRDS Directory of Mailings Lists at the library. These reference journals contain over 10,000 mailing lists with all the pertinent list data such as who owns the list, the cost, number of records, etc.

Q. What's the most valuable sheet of paper in all of direct marketing?

A. A letter. If you don't include a letter in your direct mail package you could be losing up to 40% of your response. Make it look like a letter. At a printing cost of 1-1/2 cents, it's cheap insurance to make your package work harder.

Q. If a letter is so strong in direct mail, do I need a brochure?

A. You should have a brochure or better yet a booklet. This is used to build credibility for your letter and offer. The brochure tells, the letter sells. Show the features your products have in the brochure, and the benefits of those features in the letter.

Q. What's the most effective campaign in direct marketing?

A. That would be mailing a series of 6 to 12 letters to your top 100 prospects. If you're with a large firm, mailing to your top 500 or 1,000. If you're with a really large firm, having each of your top sales personnel mail to their top 100.

Press Relations

Q. What's the most valuable sheet of paper in all of marketing?

A. A Press Release is the single most effective single sheet of paper in all of marketing. A press release is a one page, double spaced, typed sheet of paper with a description of your product or service written in a crisp, concise newspaper-style of writing. It is sent to editors of newspapers and magazines and - if selected to be published - it is printed as editorial.

Q. Should I send a letter with my press release? Why should I say "Enclosed is a press release..." they can see it's a press release when they open it.

A. Does Captain Hook have a wooden leg? You bet! A letter builds credibility, subtly explains why the press release should be published, and supplies additional material you might not be able to say your release that an editor can also pick up and use if your press release is published.

Q. How many press releases do I send out in a medium-sized campaign?

A. At our small firm (2 of us) we send out a medium-sized campaign to about 100 newspapers and magazines. We try to do this every week - we don't always meet this goal, but we always try.

Q. What are the chances of our press release being published?

A. Small trade magazines: 10 to 20%. Larger trade magazines: 5 to 10%. Consumer magazines: 1% It's like shaking hands with the Pope - it can happen, but not without a lot of effort.

Q. How can I increase my chances of having my press release published?

A. Call the editor. When you call the editor, you increase your chances by 50%. When you place an ad, your chances of having a press release run can as high as 90% - if you go about it the right way. ("If I place this ad, do you think I can have a press release run in the next issue?")

*This article about product marketing has
been customized for the book industry*

FINDING MARKETS FOR YOUR BOOKS THROUGH MAGAZINES

No matter what kind of book you're publishing, chances are good that magazines can help you reach your targeted reader audience. How do you find the right periodicals and what steps should you take when you've found them? Stick around for some answers.

Start by finding the wonderful marketing reference tools of magazine directories. They're at the library reference desk... and have names like Bacon's Magazine Directory, SRDS Business Publication Advertising Source™, and Oxbridge Communications Directory of Periodicals.

In the front of each directory you'll find you'll quickly become a marketing expert by simply reading the 2 or 3 page "market classification section" of these giant yet simple-to-use 2500-3000 page media directories. The marketing section in each directory is short, yet it presents a comprehensive list of specific "markets" or "industries" that groups of magazines are sent to. Examples of market classifications would be "photography," "motorcycles," "banking and finance," or "women's interests."

So, step one in your marketing plan is to write down any and every market classification (or marketing category) that is likely to appeal to potential purchasers of your book. There are about 100 market classifications in all, some are broken down into several subsections or market segments.

The two or three page marketing classification section gives you the page number of where the magazines can be found in the main section of the directory. The main section - thousands of pages - lists all the magazines by classifications you just saw in the front of the book. This alphabetical listing groups of all the banking magazines under "B", and the group of all the dentists' magazines are found under "D".

So, after you find the markets for your product, turn to the page shown in the main section of the directory and see the complete listing of all the magazines for that particular market classification. If your products were marketed to accountants, you'd find all the magazines that went to accountants in the beginning of the main section in any of the directories under the classification "Accounting." There's probably about 50 titles or so of magazines that go to the accounting industry.

You see, each of the directories – they're all the same in this regard - all the magazines that go to a specific industry are grouped together in the main section. For example, In Bacon's Directory for the classification of "photography," all 50 photography magazines (28 professional & 22 consumer) can be found starting on page 2207 under the title "Photography". So, go to page 2207 and you'll find all the photography magazines in alphabetical order and a complete breakdown of publisher, who they are targeted to reach (consumers, professionals, wedding, journalists, wildlife, studio, beginners, pro, semi-pro, high end, portrait, commercial - and you thought there was only one!), their editorial profile, the circulation, advertising costs, editors' names and of course their audience profiles.

That's the best part: each magazine write-up contains an editorial profile statement - who specifically the magazine is written for – or for you technical people out there, the "marketing segment" or "niche" - within the market classification. Read the profiles and make a list of the magazines that target your specific reader audience. There, that was simple. A good part of your marketing is now finished. But don't grab that beer and turn on the TV just yet...

Next? Here's where the real marketing begins. You need to analyze the markets - and you start by getting copies of all the magazines.

Since you never, ever should place an ad in a magazine you haven't seen, you're going need sample copies. Call the publisher and ask for the advertising sales department. Tell the space rep that you're thinking about buying ad space in the magazine and you'd like a "media kit" and a couple of recent issues. While you're on the phone, also ask for a copy of any circulation bureau audit reports so you will have a confirming, detailed breakdown of circulation. All the larger publishers subscribe to an independent auditor who verifies there publishing numbers. Don't believe anything about pass around copies - it's a fabricated number no one really knows about. Also remember, the number sent isn't necessarily the number read. Think about all the magazines on your desk you never got to, and finally threw them all out.

I also always ask whether the magazine has a directory issue or special annual issue, and if it does I request it and advertising rates for it. These special issues can show you a lot about a publication's strength and its depth of knowledge of the industry it serves. It can also be an extraordinarily valuable resource to you.

It's best to begin by writing and sending press releases, because when your press releases are published, they're published for free. If your press release is published and draws a profitable response from a particular magazine or better yet, market segment, and you sell a lot of books, you may find direct response ads in those publications may be cost-effective. But be careful: it can be tough to make a $25 book pay for itself with a space ad. Since this is a long shot, don't test the waters with a heavy ad schedule up front. Place ONE ad and see if the draw is anywhere close to break even. If it is, you can always go back and place more ads. If it isn't close, even the repetition of several ads won't bring you up to profitability.

Figuring the payout is simple. If your book retails for $25 (and costs you $5 to print, so you net $20) and the ad costs $600, you need to sell 30 books to break even, if S&H washes out. ($20 net x 30 books = $600).

If the magazine is an ideal target market niche, you may want to think about pitching an article derived from your book and/or an interview with you to the editorial staff. Write a one-page query letter to the editor about an article placement. Or if you like the telephone, simply call the editor and pitch.

Now's the time to mail press releases to your target market.

If you've selected three or four industries or "market classifications," you might have found roughly 60 to 150 trade and consumer magazines that seem like good places to run an ad or send a press release. If your products are of more general interest, you may have a list of 400 or 500 magazines.

If you prefer, you can cover the same bases with a letter like this one sent by traditional mail or even by fax:

Gentlemen:

We are interested in a possible ad insertion schedule in your publication.

Please send your media kit for _____ magazine.

Kindly enclose two recent copies of the magazine, along with any reference issue, directory issue, or annual summary issue you may publish. Please include display and classified advertising rates.

In your correspondence, please advise us of your editorial calendar, along with the closing dates of each issue.

Please also let us know if you publish a card pack, newsletter, or similar style publication to this industry, and if advertising space is available in it. Kindly include a recent issue, also.

Thank you for your prompt response.

When you find a magazine you're almost sure to advertise in or one that you want to examine closely over time for advertising potential, ask a sales rep to start you on a complimentary subscription. Almost always, they'll agree.

Alternatively, you can simply pay for the subscription, but I never do - and here's the trick: if it's a trade magazine, fill out the reader service card in the sample copies they sent you and check the "Start my subscription" block. Don't fall for the "Get a subscription for just $29.95" post card in the magazine unless it's a consumer magazine: 95% of all trade journals are sent free to qualified recipients. Check the audit statements you receive in the media kit to see how many free subscribers they have vs. paid subscriptions.

Analyzing and Evaluating Magazines

In about two weeks you're going to have about 60 media kits and 150 magazines on your desk, or worse, on your kitchen table. As they arrive, sort them into primary, secondary, and tertiary market piles or boxes. Then evaluate them all at once.

Glance through every media kit; remove the circulation statement, the rate schedule and anything else that seems useful; keep at least two copies of each magazine and the annual or directory issues and throw the rest of the contents out after glancing over it. Now, have a glass of wine. I've found magazine analysis goes better with a light Merlot.

Many of the magazines will show two circulation figures in their literature -- their actual circulation, as found on their audit statements, and what they usually call their "pass-along readership" or "pass-along circulation." Remember that the first circulation figure represents the number of magazines sent out; I believe the number of people who actually read each issue is smaller. And take the pass-along number with a grain of salt. Every magazine touts a pass-along copy audience, but there's no way to measure it accurately if at all.

Publishers also fail to mention some issues - like June, July, and August - don't get read at all, as their potential readers are all at the beach or outside having fun. Actual readership generally falls off significantly in the summer.

Read the magazines that serve your primary markets not only to evaluate them, but also to look for similar products and your competitors' ads. If it's a glossy, four-color coffee table magazine with lots of four-color ads, will the black-and-white ad you can afford look lost or reflect poorly on you, your product and your company?

If you find ads for a competing products, ask the magazine sales rep how long and how often they've been running in the magazine. If those ads have been appearing for a while, they're probably working, and this magazine should start to look more attractive to you for your own ad.

If you have any doubts about the editorial content aligning with profiles of your own customers, call the editorial department and ask who reads the publication. If the market isn't a good match for your titles, you usually have a better chance of finding out from an editor than from a space salesperson. In fairness, some space salespeople are truly honest and capable of supplying you with in-depth industry media assessment, and will tell you even if their own media mix isn't right for your advertising.

Final Selection

Lots of magazines will fit in with your product marketing to some extent. Your mission, should you decide to accept it, is to determine the markets and magazines within those markets with the absolute best fit: the ones that make it most likely you'll get maximum qualified responses and sales from an ad or press release.

Still have those sample magazines? Good. On the cover of each one, in big black numbers, write the cost of whatever ad you think you might buy (full-page black-and-white, one-third-page, one-fourth-page, whatever) and the circulation. Also, note whether the magazine accepts press releases and, if it does, write down the name of the column that prints releases. Put a post-it note on that column's page and post-it notes on pages with competitors' ads.

If a magazine isn't right for an ad or press release, keep just the cover. In six months, when you're wondering if you've reviewed that publication or not, you'll have a record of it. A thin record.

Now separate magazines for advertising consideration and magazines for press releases or editorial pitches only. If you need an ad, most magazines will layout an ad for you if you contract for placement of the ad. Make sure the ad composition isn't given to an intern, and ABSOLUTELY NEVER RUN AN AD YOU HAVEN'T SEEN... AND APPROVED, even if you're up on deadline. There is ALWAYS next month. Always.

Now, you can mail your press releases. The results will tell you how well you did your research. If you're successful, at the conclusion of your campaign you'll be counting the book sales and money.

Pre- and Post-Tradeshow Mailers

As a direct marketing guy I've always considered trade shows as my second least favorite way of marketing, the first being the phone. Why should I pick up the phone and call a dozen people in an hour, when I can send out four thousand letters in the same amount of time and never have to face any more rejection than the usual "Not tonight dear, I have a headache," from my wife.

But some of my clients seem to need that face time, that one-on-one with prospects. These are the clients that seem to live in a world of yesteryear: where there was no Internet, no fax machines. Some of my clients seem to even pre-date color brochures, let alone print-on-demand printing presses. They go back to the days prospective purchasers had no way to view a vendor's image other than what they were wearing when they showed up at the prospect's doorstep: a suit and tie.

Maybe that's what I hate so much, wearing a tie. What a useless garnish of clothing unless you are going to a hanging, and it's your own. So it all comes out now. Anyhow, I still hate tradeshows, old clients, ties, writing, this computer I'm typing on, and yes, I'm the guy who shot your dog in the butt from the just-slightly-open-window-on-the-third-floor with my BB gun after he crapped on my lawn and you didn't clean it up. OK, I've come clean. Where is my analyst when I really need him?

But still, some clients not only like trade shows, they thrive on trade shows as a lifeblood of their marketing, ridiculous as it may seem. So here are some direct marketing tips to make trade shows even more effective.

The Pre-show mailer: A letter is fine, so is a post card. Mail two weeks before the first day of the show, to arrive in your prospects' hands a week before the show. Mail first class. Don't use a label, they look cheap. Always have. And you know that cheap suit you bought a few years ago and said "maybe no one will notice?" They do. It looks cheap, too. Get a new one.

About your pre-show mailer - don't worry, they'll read it. At a week before the show, attendees are committed to going - and it's probably costing their firm a few thousand dollars to get them there and put up with them, er... put them up. So, at this point they'll read anything that's show related. It won't be until the third day of walking the show floor that they'll be sick of the show, the products - yes even your's, the rubber chicken lunches or the $9 dollar hot dogs they find at the convention center, and they'll be truly disinterested in any mail you send them.

Mail to a list of attendees, less exhibitors. If unavailable, mail to attendees and exhibitors. Still no dice? Mail to last year's attendees. Still no luck attaining the list? You're not really going to a trade show, are you? You just told your boss that, didn't you? Quit going to those cheap x rated shows during working hours... you can get that stuff online. Call me for the best URLs.

Get your mailer opened by using the best teaser copy for any envelope or mailer: "Gift Certificate Enclosed." Gift certificates make for ideal letter-opening teaser copy, plus they're inexpensive to print and light to ship. Redemption value can be revealed inside the package, or at the show booth. This is a great line to get any of your mail opened, and it's copyrighted by me, Jeff Dobkin: send me ten bucks every time you use it or I'll sue.

The objective of your letter or post card should be to drive people to your booth the first day or two - or... or... remember paragraph 6 about the third day? Make an nice offer - give something away. Don't make the same mistake I did - I tried to give away my wife. Not only didn't people come to my booth,

I kept the entire isle clear. Eventually on the way home I got a bottle of wine for her. It was a pretty good trade.

At one show a client of mine gave away Cross Pens, and it was a pretty successful promotion for both of us. The Cross Pens drove even the most elusive upscale prospects to his booth - so it was successful for him. I charged him three grand for the campaign, so it was successful for me. We were both happy.

To give the pen out I wrote in the Johnson box of our pre-show letter (upper right corner of the sheet, above the salutation) "If your award number: JD-122446" (printed on its own line in a rubber-stamp-looking font,) "matches the winning number: 'JD-122446' then Congratulations! You have won a beautiful new CROSS PEN! Please bring this letter with you to our booth and pick up your new Cross Pen during show hours!" No one knew that everyone won, not even our exhibit staff.

Unfortunately we ran out of a thousand dollars worth of Cross pens the first hour. So, we bought the entire stock of Cross Pens at the local office supply stores - and gave them out during the second hour... Then we finally gave up on the instant gratification we had hoped to provide along with our sales pitch, and gave out rain checks -- and mailed pens a few days later to the other few hundred letter-waving tradeshow booth visitors clinging to our promotional piece in their sweaty little hands.

Other pre-show ideas: Mail something bulky to get prospects' attention. Mail a golf ball to each attendee - and have them try to shoot 3 holes in 1, and win $100. Send a Frisbee, have them toss it into a round hole cut into a basketball backboard about 20 feet away - three times in a row for $1,000. Cut the hole 1" too small. Ha, ha ha. Oops, just kidding. Cut the hole 2" larger in the center to accept the Frisbee. It looks easy because of the big round hole, but the Frisbee will only fit in the exact center. People who miss get to keep a Frisbee. Now they're walking around with your ad.

Post show mailings: Don't give expensive literature out during the show: what a waste, it just gets sandwiched in a plastic bag between everyone else's literature - to be looked at sometime between later and never and it usually gets the briefest glance or more likely just winds up being thrown out. Mail your trade literature on the last day of the show to the people who stopped at your booth. This shows attendees you're on the ball, and you'll be a responsive team to work with.

Personalize the letter you send with your literature because you met the person. Act civil - like you had a meaningful relationship with them in the 7 minutes or so you took to speak with them at your booth. Don't write to the woman who you took to dinner and ahemmm... In fact, don't even give her your business card: give her someone else's card you picked up at the show. For this reason I always get a few cards from my competitors...

"We send our literature - along with a personal letter — to arrive 2 days after the show closes. It lands on their desk without lots of competing literature while the show is still fresh in their minds." Says Carb.

"I instruct my clients to do the same," says Jeff Dobkin, author of this article. "But in reality, who knows when they send it out, if they ever do." I hope your marketing team is run in a more timely fashion.

The sales team gets the hot leads for immediate follow-up, and the soft leads are placed in a prospect or suspect database for subsequent mailings. I recommend that you send several letters to attendees over the period of a few months. Our post-show mailing pattern is package #1-immediate, #2-two weeks, #3-four weeks, #4-eight weeks. All contain personal letters, usually with, but sometimes without a brochure for a more personal feel. The tone is always personal - if you really do it right, no one will suspect you are sending the same personal letter to the other 2,000 people who stopped at your booth.

Remember, one overbearingly long follow-up letter is usually tossed out, but the same three or four pages of material make three or four great one-page letters. For two dollars and four cents in postage you can send a series of six letters to a highly qualified prospect. And I recommend it.

Sounds like a good pre- and post-show program. Hey, if this works for you - send me a bottle of Champagne, will you? And quit walking your dog in front of my house - it would be pretty easy to shift my site up a few inches and a little to the left.

HOW TO FIGURE OUT IF YOUR MAILING WILL MAKE MONEY *BEFORE* MAILING IT.

The best way to get more customers is to mail them something like a new tie or a 10 pound box of Godiva Chocolate. Right? But those gifts aren't really feasible, are they? No, I didn't think so.

I agree, direct mail is one of the best ways to get customers. So how about if we simply mail potential customers a few nice letters, or a few post cards? Yes, that's still one of the most effective marketing campaigns.

When you know your target market, you can minimize your marketing expense by mailing just to your most likely prospects. Here, direct mail really rocks. The more focused and targeted your mailing list is, the better (= less costly, more orders per pieces mailed) your mailing works.

Conversely, when your market (your most likely customers), isn't a well-focused group, when they are not easily defined or are strewn across several boundaries, then direct mail probably won't work. You can't mail to everyone - it's way too expensive. Let's take a closer look at the costs, and see if we can figure out how to determine if your mailing will be successful before you spend any money.

Rule number one: A mailing (letter and brochure) to a group of prospects will cost you roughly half dollar for each piece.

Face it. It's 41¢ just for postage, plus the list can run 10¢ for each name and address record. Plus envelope, letterhead, brochure, add to that mailshop services to put it all together, and presto: it's expensive.

What does all this mean? It means if you mail out 1,000 pieces, it's gonna cost you $500. If your list is 5,000 names, it'll cost you $2,500 to mail to everyone on it; and if you're mailing to 10,000 prospects it'll cost you $5,000. Five grand! Wow.

Here's the upside: suppose your test mailing works and you make money? Suppose you mailed 1,000 pieces and you made $750? Then you mailed 10,000 pieces and made $7,500? Now you can roll out and mail to the rest of the list. If the list is 2,000,000 records, well - you do the math. But, I'm getting ahead of myself.

Some people say direct mail is expensive, some say it's cheap. Your point of view comes from how much income you make on each mailing. And that will depend on your A) response rate, and B) your gross revenue - and C) your gross profit per sale. Here's how to figure it all out.

Gross Revenue = Your total income

Gross Profit (GP) = The money you made after you deduct the cost of goods (COG) and fulfill-ment. Also defined as total revenue less cost of goods = gross profit

Fulfillment = Cost of packaging and shipping orders

Percent Response = number of people who buy your product from the number mailed expressed as a percentage.

Rule Two: Work the numbers backwards.

To figure out if a mailing will be successful, you'll need to know what percent response you must get to show a profit. For example, let's create a test mailing of 1,000 pieces - it's easy to work with this number:

Test mailing: 1,000 pieces.
Cost of mailing: $500
Your product sells for: $100.
Product (and fulfillment) costs: $50.
Gross profit you make on each sale: $50.

How many people have to buy your product for you to break even? Answer: 10. If you had the correct answer pat yourself on the back and get a beer. Get me one, too. No TV yet, though...

Gross Profit = Money you still have in your pocket after buying the goods and shipping them to your customers.

Calculation

· Your mailing is 1,000 pieces.
· Your mailing cost (at 50¢ each) is $500.
· Your product sells for $100.
· Your product (and shipping) costs you $50
· You make $50 Gross Profit on each sale.
· At a 1% response rate, you have 10 sales.
  Ten sales is $1000 in revenue,
  Product cost and fulfillment is $500
  Gross Profit on 10 sales is $500.
    · This will cover the cost of the mailing.
· Therefore: you need a 1% response to break even.
· Anything under 1% response you lose money
· Anything over 1% response you make money

Rule Three: Use what you have learned to make money.

Now, let's get profitable. Tweak and fine tune your direct mail package and offer, to make it draw better. Get just one more person to order, and here's what happens...

If 11 people order, you make money. This is an 11% response rate and you are profitable. When the first 10 people bought your product, your gross profit ($500) covered the cost of the mailing. With the next purchaser you made $50. And every purchaser after that, you make another $50. Is it as simple as that? Yes, yes it is. At 1.5% response, 15 people order, you make $250.

Rule Four: Here's how to figure out if your mailing will be successful before you mail anything.

Just like we did above, figure out the number of people who must order for you to break even. Base your mailing costs on $500 per thousand pieces mailed: if you mail 1,000 pieces, how many units will you need to sell to cover the $500 in mailing costs? Convert that into a percent response = number of people who need to purchase. Then see if that percent is a reasonable figure.

Let's take another example. A lot of people ask me if I sell my book, How To Market A Product for Under $500, through direct mail. I tell them no. Here's why: I mail 1,000 pieces at a cost of $500. My book sells for $30, and after fulfilling each order I make $10 profit on each sale, so I'd need 50 sales (50 x $10 = $500) to cover the cost of the mailing and break even. I'd need a 5% response rate. But, I don't think I can hit that - a 5% response is very unlikely. This is why most products selling for twenty or thirty dollars won't work for solo direct mail offers. Which brings us to Rule 5:

Rule 5: Be realistic: what percent of the list of people you are mailing will order?

Traditionally, success is based on a 1/2% to 1-1/2% order rate to break even. Anything higher is unrealistic. While it may happen, it's less likely. You need to be profitable at 1/2% to 1-1/2% response.

Rule 6: Here are the real ways you make money in direct mail.

First, find a source for quality mailing lists. Next, create a mailing that's profitable - no easy task. Test products, offers, lists - this is the hardest part! Eventually if you stick with it you'll find something that tests successfully. Even if it just throws off a little cash after you pay for mailing, product and fulfillment costs, that's OK. Then, how long is the list?

DIRECT MARKETING STRATEGIES

Once your offer tests successfully and it's profitably mailing to small segments of your list, increase the size of your mailings. As larger segments of the list test successfully, you can mail to the rest of the list with similar predictable results. The percentage of people ordering should be the about the same as your test mailings. The way you make money - with little risk - is to send the same mailing piece to the rest of the people on the same list.

If you make a profit of $50 on your first test mailing of 1,000 pieces, you should make $500 on a mailing to 10,000. And $5,000 on a mailing to 100,000. How about if this list was 2.5 million records? This is the way you make money in direct mail - you duplicate your success. Make sure your mailing is scalable, because if it works in the small scale - testing - it'll work in a large scale. The same package to the same list = same results.

Finally, we're not finished making money yet from people who ordered. If you supplied a great product and great service to people who order, you're going to get additional business from them. And referrals. Your cost to get them to reorder is near zero. You're marketing to a warm market - they have become the GROUP MOST LIKELY TO PURCHASE from you.

So further mailings to this select group of purchasers will yield much better results, and cost you much less. If your purchaser list is large enough, you can just mail to them. Your response rate will soar. So will your profit. Hey, if this happens, send me something nice. My favorite color is blue, my favorite car... a Corvette. Thanks.

MARKETING WITH POST CARDS

The absolute best campaign you can create is a letter campaign. A series of personalized letters sent over time can be your most effective selling tool, ever. But man, they're a lot of work.

So the problem is: how can you stay in your customers' Top-of-Mind-Awareness without all that work. The answer is: with a few post cards. By mailing post cards to each prospect or customer every three to eight weeks, your customers and prospects think of you when they need something, and pick up the phone and call you when they're ready to buy.

Post cards are hard working marketing tools because...

They're cheap to produce.

Since a post card is usually a single sheet of paper, it's always cheaper than sending a letter and a brochure stuffed into an envelope. Post cards also incur no lettershop charges of folding and inserting: just image a name and address on one side and away they go.

The postage is cheaper, too.

They're cheap to mail first class: just 26¢ each. This cost is before any postal discounts, which can be substantial! Strangely enough, post cards can be cheaper to mail FIRST CLASS than bulk. Restrictions apply - they must be bar-coded and carrier-route labeled, which is done routinely if you use a lettershop to sort and mail.

Need fast delivery of your message?

Mailing post cards allows you to take advantage of first class delivery while enjoying the postage savings from the first class letter rate.

Postal savings even when mailing just a few cards.

Is your mailing list just to a few hundred special people? Even when just mailing a few handfuls, post cards under 4-1/4" x 6" have a lower postage rate than first class letters: 26¢ - even without any discounts.

Mailing house costs can be completely offset by postage savings.

Tired of doing it yourself? If you take your post cards to a mailing house, their entire cost of inkjet addressing, tying, bagging and delivering to the post office may still cost you less than if you mailed them yourself. It's like getting their service for FREE. You save money because their payment is recovered from all of the postal discounts they get for you. It's a win-win-win: you have less work, save money, and you get better delivery.

Post cards have high readership.

Almost everyone reads post cards, even the good folks who throw out all your bulk direct mail! Heck, all the wording is... right there! By the time your customers have it in their hands... they're reading it.

They're diverse.

Post cards can be looked at as a piece of one-to-one communication - so you can be as personable as "jest settin' on your front stoop," or as formal as a bound book with an embossed gold leaf cover.

Post cards can come back to haunt you.

Double post cards are great as a response vehicle. Many double post cards test profitably against long-copy packages on subscription offers, especially where the magazine is well known. As a bonus, since the address side already contains the customer name, along with any marketing data you'd like to see, it's possible to use that card as a pre-filled-out order card the customer just drops in the mail.

Post cards handle illustrations well.

Line art, airbrush, four color - even crayon... whatever you have, it can look great on a post card. Better paper stock enhances the "It didn't come out as good as we thought it would!" designs.

They're inexpensive to print - no need to go four color.

A nice thing about post cards - one or two color post cards work just fine, and they're cheaper to print. About 90% of the post cards I create for clients are specified to be printed in just one or two colors.

Four color post cards are cheap to have printed.

There are some gang-run post card printers (no, not that kind of gang - post cards are printed en masse on giant sheets of 24" x 26" post card paper stock, then trimmed) and the cost can be as low as $350 for 5,000 cards. Call Postcard Power 800-411-6256 (www.postcardpower.com) for their free catalog, or 800POSTCARDS (www.1800postcards.com.). Or try Modern Postcard (www.modernpostcard.com), call 800-959-8365 and ask for their free sample kit. Or call Mitchell Graphics, 800-583-9401, for samples and pricing, or Simply Postcards: 800-770-4102. Tell them Dobkin sent you.

They're easy to handle.

Doing the mailing yourself? No stuffing, no folding.

Not much messing around - just print, address, and mail.

Another use for post cards: Need to get undeliverable names and addresses mailed back so you can remove them from your mailing list?

Need to make address corrections in a timely fashion without additional expense? Send post cards first class with the imprint "Address Service Requested" below the stamp: the post office will return cards with undeliverable addresses back to you. Lots of catalog companies do this before mailing their catalog - it's much cheaper to get cards back for free than to pay for getting wrecked and unusable catalogs back after the rough handling by the postal service.

Need a quick survey response?

Keep post card surveys short, and ask recipients to fax them back. There's a good chance you'll get lots of them returned.

Additional Recommendations

There are three hard and fast recommendations for post cards. First, don't use cheap paper. Since post cards are usually small sheets, go for the good stuff. In short runs, paper stock is a small fraction of the overall costs. I never recommend cheap paper for anything but the cheapest promotions from my cheapest clients, and sometimes for longer press runs of 25,000 sheets and up - where paper cost is a much larger percentage of the overall campaign costs.

Second, don't go for gloss unless you are printing in four colors. A glossy finish will get marked, mangled and scarred at the post office - gloss cards aren't handled well by the automatic equipment at the post office. Chances are your glossy post card will be delivered with the equivalent of an 18 wheeler tractor trailer skid mark across the billboard side, and hard telling what the address side will look like. The paper stock I recommend? A crisp, bright-white 80 pound linen stock.

Third, don't go for the smallest size card - like the standard card the post office offers. The minimum size card doesn't scream out for attention like a 5-1/2" x 8-1/2" card does, which is the size I recommend. The largest size you can mail without incurring additional expense (over 26¢) is 4-1/4" x 6". The largest post card size you can mail for first class letter postage of 41¢ is an 8-1/2" x 11" sheet. If you can't make a lasting impression with that size, call me and let's talk.

Examples of successful campaigns

An insurance client of mine needed a post card that would be retained by the customer, or at least until their present insurance expires (their ex-date). Theory was: then they'd have the card on-hand and would call him for a quote. We created a 3-fold (21" x 5-1/2" folded to 7" x 5-1/2") card printed in bright yellow and black with the words "SEND HELP" on one side, and with a "what to do in case of an accident" report form on the back. His first run was 10,000. Results: 3 more runs of 10,000 each over the next 6 months. Everyone loved them. They're in everyone's glove compartment. We said "save this card" on each and everyone did. We also printed "Call us for fast friendly information or a quick quote on rates," and everyone did that, too.

An interim placement specialist in the financial community sends post cards every 4 to 6 weeks to his client list. His objective: Top-of-Mind Awareness. Eight years ago when we started he had a mailing list of 250. Now he mails to over 1,200 a month. We're now working on his 36th card (we repeated our favorites over several mailings). Whenever he speaks with clients they always mention they enjoy his cards. The copy on one of my favorite cards: "When your loan manager goes on leave does your customer service follow suit?" He's famous in his industry for his post cards.

Creating successful cards is easy:

On the billboard side: as you would for any advertisement, design for 3 levels of readership: 1. a big BOLD HEADLINE to entice scanning readers. This copy is for folks who just glance at your card to get the idea. If you entice them with a clever headline, they'll continue reading. Your headline has one objective: drive the reader into the rest of the copy.

2. SUBHEADS are then written and designed to intrigue and arouse the reader further. This is the "not quite as large as the headline type, and not quite as small as the body copy type" line that encourages the smooth transition between

the two areas. This line also has the same objective as the headline: get customers to read further.

3. The first line or two of the body copy must be smart and sharp - written and designed from the getgo to fulfill the specific objective of... keeping the reader reading. The complete transition of a scanning reader to a confirmed reader still hasn't taken place yet.

After the first few clever lines in your body copy, the reader is then hooked: he's made a commitment to read the rest. Now you can start selling your post card objective whether it is to 1. generate an inquiry via phone by having readers call for further information, 2. generate an order directly from the card, 3. get them to come into your retail store, or 4. send (write or fax) for more information. Don't forget to tell the reader exactly what you want him to do, and be specific.

Additional Tips:

At the bottom of the post card your logo may be the same size but certainly no larger than your telephone number, which should be big enough to see clearly if the card is laying on a desk and a cataract patient is trying to dial your number while standing there with a phone in one hand.

Always print "Save this card!" somewhere near the top, and people will. It's funny - if you don't print this line, they won't.

It's OK to send a card more than once. Successful cards can be sent forever as long as they continue to successfully cover their costs. Unsuccessful cards or cards tougher to track can still be sent regularly. You get sick of looking at your cards long before your customers get tired of receiving them. If any customers complain, hey - you're getting noticed.

Traditional post cards - those small manila cards you can buy at the post office - may be used for technical, reference-only mailings to engineers and computer geeks. If you want a reference-looking card almost like the one the government would put out notifying you of a tax lien, this is the one. If you sell softwear, "Now shipping version 4.3" doesn't necessarily need to be in full color.

Also, if your sole intention is to notify a broad customer base of a technology change or B2B product (perhaps as unglamorous as your launch of a new ball bearing, or other necessary product information) as cheaply as possible, the standard manila cards the post office issues will work here, too. But if you're selling something the least bit upscale, or want to command attention, use a larger card of better quality paper.

Double post cards are good for feedback. Besides the larger area for image and copy, you can get an easy-to-use response vehicle in the same piece of mail. This format of cards is great and tests well for well-known and re-up magazine and newsletter subscriptions. They also are good for purging your database of old names and bad addresses, and for asking recipients for recommendations for new names and gathering addresses for mailing and email lists.

Getting your card back

While double post cards are the norm, if you're not die-cutting one side for the address to show through, it's always a problem figuring out which side to address, which is the billboard side, and which side to address to get it back to you.

There are a few alternatives: first, consider a triple post card: three cards scored and folded over to the size of one card. For the little extra it costs for the small square of paper and the extra fold, you get a third more selling space, and it's cheaper than a diecut. It's also much easier to design a dedicated return card that doesn't have to double as something else.

Alternatively, you can leave the return address side with an address grid the recipient fills out before sending back. If your computer printer can print a name and address upside down - you can print the recipient's name and address and/or any priority or special coding in the upper right-hand corner of the return card above the address grid. This is above the fold. Below the fold is the address side to whom you are sending the card. This eliminates inkjetting on the second (back) side of the card in a separate inkjet pass. It's an exceptionally easy-to-use return-card format.

With a single card you can have recipients fill out a few questions in a survey, then fax the whole card back to you. This type of card is great for surveys - which I believe are one of the most under-used types of promotions. When you engage a client in a survey, it can be a cleverly disguised promotional piece designed to increase your brand awareness, feel customers out to see if they're ready to buy, or entrench your advertising message more firmly into their mind. But, that's another article...

Bring in some visual recognition

When creating a multi-card campaign, keep the image and the message the same on the address side of each succeeding card. It's usually institutional copy anyhow on this side - name, address, phone, blah blah blah. The address side is also a good place for a few bold lines or a free offer to the reader to get more information: "Call now to get our free booklet about ____."

As with any campaign of repeated exposures, your logo plays a an important part of your visual identity. Your mark should be strong enough so that someone who sees it the first time, remembers it the second time, and each time thereafter.

Don't forget - a post card campaign is not a single mailing, a campaign by definition is a sustained effort over time, so mail frequently. And above all: it's direct mail and direct mail is always a game of numbers - mail as many cards to as many people as you can.

10 MORE TIPS ON CREATING EFFECTIVE POST CARDS

Hi. Jeff Dobkin here. You remember me, old guy who is cranky when he wakes up and then it all goes downhill from there. Bum knee, bald spot and can't eat sugars. Of course, I'm ranked 4th in Pennsylvania in racquetball and I dirtbike most every weekend. Go ahead - try and keep up.

The post card is an anomaly in the postal system. You can actually mail a post card first class cheaper than you can mail it bulk rate. In addition, you can get post cards imprinted with an address and a bar code and save more in postage costs than you pay for this addressing service. Delivery is one to three days.

What I like best about post cards is by the time the reader decides to toss it out, he's already read it. No getting around it, readership can be extremely high for a well designed card.

For post cards to be effective, some rules apply.

1. AIDA. Attract Attention, Interest the reader, show something they Desire, and Ask for Action. One of the few remaining places this old advertising acronym still works.

2. Don't sell anything. A post card is too short for a sales pitch. The objective is simple: make an offer to Generate a phone call.

Here's how:

3. Show a bold headline that interests the reader. Want an effective formula to create a winning headline? Here it is: Write 50 headlines, go back and pick out your best one. Hey,

I didn't say you'd like it - I just said it would be effective. Go on: write 50. I'll wait.

4. OK, start writing. So what if it takes you 2 days. What are you waiting for? Go on... just start.

5. Still no luck writing? Need help? OK, here's a hint: offer a FREE BOOKLET. Free offers get readers to call, and... HEY! That's the objective of the card.

6. The TITLE of the booklet drives the reader to call. So make it a great one, information everyone MUST have. Here's how: Write 100 titles, then go back and pick out your best one. And you complained about writing 50 headlines... this'll teach you not to complain.

7. Keep copy tight and crisp. Make it look easy to read, even if it isn't. Edit it. Then edit it again. Then go back and take out 1/3 more words. What? You can't? Send it to me (hard copy, please) - I have a big red pen and I'm not afraid to use it...

8. Spend time or money or both on the billboard side. You have 2 seconds of your reader's undivided attention before your card gets thrown out - best use it wisely. Create an awesome headline. Make your free booklet offer stand out. Then, bulleted lists work well. Short blocks of copy work well also.

Break up copy by using subheads (smaller bold headlines) above every few paragraphs. Readers will scan these so keep them interesting. Direct the readers eyeflow to go exactly where you want.

6. Above all, interest the reader and keep him reading. Once the reader loses interest he stops reading, and the card gets tossed out. Interest must be immediate - and sustained - as the reader is still standing over the, ummm, round file.

7. I don't recommend 4 color. There are too many 4-color cards out there and with this market way over-saturated with them, they lose effectiveness. Print in 1 or 2 colors.

Use upscale stock. Don't use glossy stock, postal equipment rollers leave black marks.

8. Use a graphic. Your logo or graphic is a visual hook so readers remember your first card when you send the second one. Not too big, though.

9. Design with type. Spend time on design, and typography. Forget stock photography, spend your whole art budget here. The money you save from not hiring an illustrator will more than pay for itself when you spend it on a great, over-the-top graphic designer.

10. Have a big phone number. Old people should be able to read it when the card is at arm's length or sitting on a desk.

Recap: Keep it short, crisp and easy to read. Big bold headlines and offer something FREE to get readers to call and have a big phone number. The only objective is to call - measure every line of copy against this objective - does this line make people call or not?

The most effective direct mail campaign:

A letter is the most effective piece of mail for generating a phone call, but a post card isn't bad either if you have a short selling proposition and offer something for FREE.

Post cards campaigns are most effective for staying in "Top of Mind" awareness campaigns when mailed every 4 to 6 weeks. Intersperse with letters every so often and you have the best campaign ever. Any questions?

The First in Series of Articles on Successful Retail Marketing

BRINGING TRAFFIC IN YOUR FRONT DOOR.

Retailers, Storefronts and Service Business Owners - You Gotta Be Crazy! Why in the world would you want to go into retail? Did the long hours attract you? Was it spending all day in a 20- by 40-foot room that sounded so good? Or was it "never being able to go away on vacations" that drove you to opening your own retail business?

What? A restaurant? Wait then, let me guess: you wanted to own a restaurant so the thought of "prosper or die by how good your last meal is" drives you to open your doors each morning, a? Or tell me, was it getting up at 4AM so you could be the first at the wholesale produce market to get the best vegetables that appealed to you? Or having everything rely on a cranky chef? Exactly what continues to make you want to prepare fresh food for the elite group of customers who continue to eat there and yet still complain?

And hey, you in the service business, not so fast, buddy: While arrogant people with the breath of kerosene don't show up at your door, you've got to show up at theirs. You know who I mean - the ones that want you to quote every little job six ways to China, then demand you take $100 off their $200 bill once the job is completed. Yes, I get my share of those customers, too. Don't we all?

The resolution is to get more customers, and get better customers, so you can pick and choose who you want to deal with. Tell the cranky customers if they really don't like it, don't come back, or better yet - visit the Northern most parts of the United States - as my Italian friend Carlo calls it, "Uppa U.S.!" Just a few thousand words from now you can have the luxury to bid really high on jobs you don't want - so at least if you get them, they'll be worth dealing with the irate, the nasty, and the smelly-breath people who seem to have nothing better to do than stand over you and complain.

Nice dream? Yea, I guess so. But face it:

Business is lousy. The economy is tanked. "Poised for growth," is what the government says — when we're in a recession like this. And the Fed can't lower the prime rate any more or they'll be paying us to borrow money. I know, that's not what you're thinking. You're looking around your store and saying, "Where is everybody?"

Good News: If you're a retailer, here's how to get people to show up at your door. If you're in a service business, here's how to get your phone to ring. If you're a restaurateur, here's my phone number: 610-642-1000 - I usually get hungry around 7PM. If the campaign works really well, I'll be bringing a few friends.

The very first part of the campaign - as with all advertising or marketing campaigns - you have track the response of anything you do. A nasty little necessary part of any campaign is to learn what's working, and just as important, what isn't.

Without accurate tracking, you won't be able to make intelligent (= less costly) decisions about which parts of the campaign to stop and which ones to continue. You need to track response to determine what media you'll use again because it's most effective (= you made money.) Without tracking, you won't be able to figure out what worked, what didn't work - and to what extent - and exactly how many people and how much revenue each part of the campaign brought in. So reliable tracking must be built into each campaign.

I'll try to make this tracking business as painless as possible, because... well, it is. It's easy to track response if you know this simple trick: leave a memo pad by each phone and when you receive a call - in the very beginning of the conversation - say, "And how did you hear of our company/store?" Write down the response on the memo pad, along with the customer's name and any other information you can capture, and throw that slip of paper in a drawer and forget about it. At the end of the month tally them up and you'll have a pretty darn good idea which ads or campaigns brought in the most customers.

With the customer's names on each tracking sheet you'll be able to figure out which campaign brought in the best quality of customers - and no they're not all the same. With tight tracking you can even figure out how much each customer (from which source) brought in the most revenue.

The same tracking method can be used when people come into your shop or restaurant, or called you for service. Hey, instead of saying "Store, shop, restaurant or service business" and so forth in each paragraph - when I say store or shop I mean all of these, OK? Thanks.

The Campaign

Marketing options vary in effectiveness and cost from industry to industry, business type to business type, but some are definitely more effective than others across the board. I'll start with these in a loosely defined order, with the most effective at the top. So here's the first, the most effective you can be in marketing:

Mailing to your house list.

No matter what industry, what you're selling, or what type of business, restaurant or storefront you have, mailing to your house list is the lowest cost and most effective marketing you can do. Lowest cost. Most effective. Any questions?

Let's ramp this end of our marketing up. Start by collecting current customer's names and addresses. If you don't have a customer house file - a list of the names and addresses of all your customers - start one now. This will be your most valuable asset. Add fresh new names to this list every day, every week, every time you possibly can.

Whenever people come into your store, make sure you have a "Would you like to sign up for our FREE mailing list!" card by the cash register, or by the front door, or both. Don't be afraid to recommend they fill out the card.

As customers check-out, recommend the mailing list by saying that you offer special deals and private sales to pre-ferred customers. On the top of the card write "Preferred Customer" then ask for name, address, phone, email. You might offer a "$5 Gift Certificate! Good on your next visit!" as an incentive for filling out the card. I also like to ask "And where did you hear of us?" as a question on the card. Most people won't know - but a few will. Even the ones that don't know will give you a clue as to the magazines and newspaper they read.

Next, mail to your Prospect list

If you don't have a good prospect list, start one of those lists now, too. This is a database containing the name and address of the absolute best prospects you can think of. Write down the names and addresses of 5 or 6 new prospects each day and mail to them all next month. If you write 5 a day, times 20 weekdays in a month - you'll have 100 new prospect each month.

Get a customer for $.74. Send a Gift Certificate

Feel free to ask any of your better customers if they have friends they would like you to send a $5 gift certificate to, with their compliments of course. As an added incentive, mail and additional gift certificate to the first customer with a nice letter of "Thanks for the referral." Then send the referral prospect a nice letter - and of course the gift certificate - compliments of your original customer and from you, personally.

Nice campaign, isn't it. Customer acquisition cost: $.74, (postage, you know.) Then the five bucks that is taken off the goods, merchandise, or food bill didn't really cost you five bucks, did it? It was just the discounted costs of your goods.

Best of all, the $5 gift is an expense only if the customer actually shows up and redeems the gift certificate. The gift certificate campaign doesn't cost you anything if it doesn't generate a sale. So put this under a "Big Added Bonus" If no original customer comes in to claim his gift, there is no cost. And no new customer, no cost. But you still get the branding message: leaving your image by reaching and touching your original customer - and subtly reminding him of your service and how great it is. Plus, you leave a nice impression on the new prospect. A referral is the best way to get a new customer who immediately has faith and trust in you, your firm, your services.

The gift certificate is inexpensive to print and low cost to mail. The letter, same. The goodwill it generates, invaluable. It's a triple function piece. Good for the customer, good for a referral, and great for you, too.

Second in Series of Articles on Successful Retail Marketing

BRINGING TRAFFIC IN YOUR FRONT DOOR PART II.

I worked with the owner of a restaurant who blurted out over a hot cuppa coffee that since he sold food, "Everyone is a prospect". "No, don't give me that crap." I fired back. Hurmph - cheap client, only gave me coffee even when I continually showed up at lunch time sporting a lean, hungry look on my face!

While his restaurant was upscale, it wasn't "Le Fountain Bleu" and no one was going to drive an hour to eat there. So right away our target market was limited to people who lived or worked within a half hour's drive. That "market segment" qualification of our prospects was just for starters. How long people will drive to reach your business as a destination is one consideration in finding a market segment worthy of spending money to reach.

You see in marketing, everyone you reach, and every time you expose your message to someone, there is a cost associated with that contact. It's called "CPM" or "cost per thousand" - and it's the cost to reach 1,000 people with your message. Cost per Thousand. Different media have different CPM,

Reaching people with your message can get expensive in a hurry, especially if you consistently reach the wrong people - who don't care about what you're selling and who are not in the market for your goods or services.

What you are looking for in your marketing dollars is quality customers who are ready to buy. What you are looking for in an effective marketing campaign is the ability to reach the maximum number of customers who are the most qualified and are ready to buy right now. You need to reach them at the lowest possible cost and get them to call or come in by effectively delivering a message that they will respond to. Read this paragraph again, it's about as good of a solid marketing strategy as I can come up with..

Since this article is talking about retail stores, or local service providers, most of the campaigns in the article will target a geographic center. Everybody likes to shop in their own backyard. Let's look at a few campaigns, some of the figures, and how to increase their effectiveness.

Newspaper campaign

Newspapers can be a good retail tool for advertising to a specific geographic community. Here's how to make your newspaper ads more effective.

Suppose you take out an ad in a local newspaper and it costs you $100; you get 20 phone calls, and 8 people come into your place of business and 4 people purchase something. The cost per inquiry is $5 (20 calls cost you $100), the cost to acquire each customer is $25 (from your $100 ad, 4 people purchased). Well, that was easy.

Did you make any money from this campaign?

Campaigns succeed or fail depending on what customers purchase and the profit margin of each item. Using the above campaign, if you owned a car dealership you made lots of money selling four cars. But if you owned a flower shop, chances are you lost money because each sale of $20 bucks wouldn't support your initial customer acquisition cost of $25. So, to figure out if your ad is profitable (and you should keep running it) what is your AVERAGE ORDER SIZE. And how much profit do you make on this sale, after you subtract the cost of goods? (There is another piece of the puzzle, call the lifetime value of a customer, and we'll look at that in a moment.)

Now let's enhance our campaign with a more clever marketing approach. Suppose you ask each caller for their name and address - so you can send them "Invitations" to the "Private Sales" you hold several times a year. 10 prospects fork over their name and address, and you mail them a post card each month (yearly cost, 12 times 41¢ = $4.92, times 10 custom- ers = $49.20, + $26 for post cards = about $70 for the year's campaign). With this campaign, four people come in initially, but over the course of the year six more people from this list come in and buy something. Now your customer acquisition cost is $16. The actual cost for these last six customers is less than $11.00 each. That's the value of having a database of prospects and customers.

What can you afford to spend to acquire each customer?

You need to know not only how many customers call or come in, but also what customers spend as an immediate direct result of the campaign. Also, you'll need to know the annual value of a customer... and as long as we're figuring, what is the LIFETIME VALUE of a customer or "LVC". Good marketing can make a customer come in the first time, but after that - hey man, it's up to you to serve up "good value" to make them come back.

Probably the best example of this concept of a customer's annual value or lifetime value can be seen through a restau- rant owner's eyes. Patrons may spend only $30 on dinner each time they come in, but how many times a year do they eat in your restaurant? And for how many years do they stay customers? In our above example, our customer acquisition cost was $16 - which we may not have made in the first meal he ate at $30, but if the customer came in once a month for a year and spent $30 each time, our $16 acquisition cost was returned in 2 months, and we profited very well by serving him and his guest the other 10 meals throughout the rest of the year.

Knowing these statistics will allow you to figure out a budget for a cost-effective marketing plan to acquire customers.

Next time we'll look at some additional campaign examples, along with a plethora of different LOCAL advertising options including cable TV, a deeper look at newspapers, direct mail

Third in Series of Articles on Successful Retail Marketing ~

11 BEST MARKETING PRACTICES FOR RETAILERS

Here's a wish list for the retailers I work with. OK, it's MY wish list. I wish the retailers I work with would do the following:

1. Start a house mailing list

Retail... wholesale... consumer... trade - this is easily the best marketing strategy any company can establish, and it especially holds true for retailers.

Your house mailing list is your current customers; you know - the people who know where your store is, how to get there without directions, and what you stock. After they've been to your store once - if they like your selection of products and services, and the experience they had with you, they know how to get back.

There is "no-wasted-expense" in mailing to this house list of customers. Remind them of sales, new merchandise arrivals, special deals to friends, private sales, free gifts for coming back, "Thanks for your referral!" letters, post cards, coupons and warm and fuzzy personal letters. Face it: if you can't get a current customer to come back, you've done something wrong.

If you've captured their date of birth - send a b'day card. Don't forget letters and post cards for some of the smaller, lesser celebrated holidays like back to school day for kids, first day of deer season... or when trout fishing opens; ground hog's day, first blue moon of the year, etc. Don't send a card for Christmas - let everyone else send them Christmas cards, yours would get lost in the pack - who needs that?

Here's how easy it is to start a mailing list. Have a box of 3 x 5 cards near the cash register and when customers walk by, ask them to sign up for your FREE mailing list. Let them know by signing up for your (confidentially kept) mailing list they'll receive notices about private sales, special discounts, coupons, and special events. It's even easier if you have a reception desk or someone who makes appointments - it's all done at that time.

2. Have a "Best Customer" list

If you have customers that are so good, customers that visit you so frequently that you remember their names and faces, you need to put them on a preferred mailing list. These are the 100 or so best of the best (if you're a big shop, these can be 500 or 1,000 of your best). Mail them notices of private sales and events ("Only 100 of our very best customers are being invited to this very private sale..."). Make them feel special. They are.

3. Analyze your customers

The difference between marketing and sales is when you are selling, you are selling to anyone. Marketing is selling to a defined audience. When you define your audience you find the common threads that place those folks in the special group of people who want or need your services. When you discover this commonality you can then clone your customers to get more of the same. (That's why I usually look to customer's friends to become customers - they're alike, with similar interests, tastes and values.)

4. Learn how new customers heard of you

Once you find out how your customers heard of you, you can increase advertising or marketing to that medium - it's effective. Then...

5. Track your advertising

Once you find out which of your advertising works, you need to keep track - and by that I mean write it down. The simplest way for you computer geeks is to enter all this in a database. The simplest way for us normal human beings is to leave 3x5 cards next to each phone, and next to the cash register - and ask everyone who calls right there, up in the front of the conversation (or, if you're at your store, smack anyone who walks near you upside his or her head and ask) "Hey, how did you hear of us!" Write down each response on a 3 x 5 card and stash in a drawer.

At the end of the month you'll know where everyone came from. At the end of 6 months you'll know - for sure - where your advertising is working... so you can increase that part of it for next year. The other big benefit is you can drop the ineffective advertising that isn't working.

6. Have a press release program

If you said you have a good press release program, you send out a press release every year, let's talk seriously. Here's the program I like: Write down the 12 headlines for 12 press release for sending each month. Work long and hard on this. Make the headlines punchy. Use the "Jeff Dobkin 100 to 1 Rule*": write 100 go back and pick out your best one! Write and rewrite. From there, it's easy to back into the copy for the body of the release.

Once you have a tight PR headline list, over the course of the year you'll have an aggressive PR program, and you'll know exactly what release is going out, and when. That's the basic plan, but feel free to interject with a timely news release if something unusual or sensational happens in the meanwhile.

7. Create a sign

When I wrote a marketing campaign for a Realtor I discovered she received about 25% of her calls from a sign placed in front of the house. Do you have a sign in front of your store? You should. You can now buy CHANGEABLE signs fairly cheaply

- you should, and you should... change it frequently. Reason: after people see the same sign week-in and week-out they stop looking. If you change it, they look each time they pass your store. Say something right - and they'll stop in.

8. Find out where you are making the most money

Unless you are in a strong price sensitive market, increase the price point of those products and services. Then offer add-on options, and similar but more expensive products to increase your customer's average purchase. Like Sears... have you ever bought a car battery from Sears: Good, Better and Best?

This is your opportunity to be like the car manufacturers: they start most cars at a low price point, then keep adding amenities until you wind up buying a $10,000 Chrysler Neon with $9,000 in accessories. (Did you really need that 426 Hemi engine and 9-inch wide tires on that Neon?) Next year - if they sell well - the base price goes up to $12,500, and even more options are offered.

9. Find out where you are making the least money

In catalog marketing, savvy marketers use a "square inch analysis." They measure the size in square inches of the product photo and write-up, then calculate the revenue and net profit brought in by that merchandise. Then, if it isn't essential to the product mix, the merchandise with the lowest profit per square inch is dropped, and replaced with something new. This continual rotation of products is good for the overall mix and keeping the catalog profitable and costs down.

I'm not saying you should measure square footage of your store, but if some products or services are not bringing in as much net revenue for the space they are taking up, maybe it's time to rethink that product line or service.

10. Use personal letters as marketing tools

Nothing beats a personal invitation - like a letter - to an event. Nothing says "We'd really like to see you here" better than a letter with a gift certificate. Nothing is better than a personal letter to say "Thanks for being a customer, we really appreciate your business!" Even when you send a few thousand letters - if they are well written you can make the recipient feel he really special - and that he is the only person who has received it. Remember when your mom told you you were very special - and you believed her? Your customers will, too.

11. Thank customers for referrals

If a customer sends in a friend or neighbor, send them a small gift, or at least a gift certificate. Don't forget to include a nice letter with it - the value to you is not what's in the gift, but what you say in the letter. What are they likely to then do? That's right - they're likely to give you even more referrals and send in more customers. Nice.

7 Lessons in Successful Advertising

Years ago, a real estate broker hired me to help him sell more houses. We met for about 10 hours, reading over the real estate section of the paper and discussing his ads. I then told him I was ready to help him sell more houses.

"Sir!" he said in startled disbelief. "Do you mean to tell me we can meet for 10 hours and you can tell me how to sell more houses? I've been selling houses for 40 years. I've forgotten more about selling houses than you will ever learn in your life."

It was true. Too bad the reply, "Sir, I have forgotten more about advertising than you have learned in forty years of selling houses," didn't occur to me till a few weeks later – my hindsight letting me know how clever I could have been now that it's too late. But my client was right. He had forgotten quite a lot about selling houses. The structure of his entire advertising campaign was wrong. Is yours?

What my client was trying to do was sell a house in an ad. You do not sell a house in a four-line listing. No one sees the listing and sends a down payment. The correct objective of the ad was not to sell a house but to generate a phone call. If the ad worked as planned, his phone rang. It was then up to him to sell the house.

So we changed all the listings. "Call now!" the new ad copy said. "Call to see this beautiful four bedroom..." "For additional information by mail, call..." "For a free brochure with pictures of this house call us at..." and we gave the phone number. If you read all of the listings you saw that phone number dozens of times. My client's phone calls tripled, starting in week number one. The first week!

Here's the First Lesson:

Before drafting any copy for your ad, first write a clear objective to your ad.

Ask yourself, "If this ad works perfectly, what is the action-step the reader will do?" Then draft your ad to fulfill this specific objective.

Increasing Ad Response

What's the best way to get people to pick up the phone and call you? Here's a hint: offer Something for FREE. Everybody likes FREE.

Suppose you're selling the new book you've just written. How can you generate the most response from a small ad for a book? Let's see, would "Buy my new book" get readers' attention? No, not really. Unless you're Steven King, people seeing this ad aren't going to rush into a bookstore – or dive into their pocket and send you a check. So, this headline won't work. Let's go to the other extreme: Would "Get FREE MONEY!" get people excited? Yes, that's it. Now you have everyone's attention.

So the best way to generate maximum response is to give something away – for FREE. But money isn't a good giveaway because it doesn't restrict calls from just your prospects: and you don't want calls from people who just want free money, because who doesn't? These people are outside of your book's niche audience, unless of course you are writing a book about giving away free money, in which case... we should talk.

Most people who respond to "get free money" are not "the most likely immediate purchasers," which is my definition of a target market. So why waste money, literature and postage on them? Let's still give something away, but first let's make sure our FREE gift is of exceptional value... but only to our target market: people who are actively considering buying a book—such as yours.

I think the best way to attract potential customers is to give away FREE information. It's valuable to the respondent, they can't get it anywhere else, and it's cheap to produce for you - generally just a few sheets of paper and ink. Nice combo.

The information you produce should be in booklet form. In fact, "Call now for a FREE BOOKLET" is my favorite advertising headline — it promises prospects something for free, and it gives people a "reason to call." The free booklet helps overcome the law of reader inertia (a body at rest... on the couch... gets up, walks over and picks up the phone.) Additionally, to people who get flustered when they have to call somewhere new – they won't have to figure out what to say when you answer the phone, they can just ask for their FREE booklet. You may not think this is important, but it's a big factor with folks who have problems calling anyone other than friends.

Don't have a booklet? How about dressing up your new brochure as a helpful educational and information-rich resource guide? Just a few pieces of paper can become a powerful sales tool when talked about in this regard. Brochures are so passé!

Face it: a sheet of paper folded in thirds is a brochure. And you can get them anywhere: Chevy agency, bank, post office – there's just no value in an advertising brochure. But that same piece of paper folded in half... well – that becomes a valuable informational booklet. Would you rather receive a company's advertising brochure, or a free informational booklet? Yea, me too.

Lesson number 2:

Offer something for FREE to make people pick up the phone.

This was the objective of your advertisement. You do remember the objective, don't you?

Here's a big bonus for you: when people call to ask for something free, they are generally in a pleasant and giving mood – after all they're getting something for FREE. When they call for their free booklet, you can take that opportunity to poke around for the information you need from them in your own marketing. That's the time to qualify each caller as a serious prospect, a literature collector or someone with a phone and nothing better to do. So...

Lesson 3: Qualify the prospect on the incoming phone call.

Qualifying Prospects

When someone responds to an ad by calling and asking me to send information, my next words rarely—if ever—are "OK, what's your address?" Instead, I ask probing questions designed to qualify prospects (i.e., figure out how likely they are to buy, and when). "I'd be happy to send you this FREE booklet; say, where did you see our ad..."

Frankly, the qualification process starts much sooner than when you speak with a prospect. You initially qualify response by deciding in which publications to run your ad. Whatever audience your chosen medium reaches is the start of your qualification process. Looking for camera buffs? Camera magazines. Airplane aficionados? Modern Flyer Magazine. Looking for beautiful women under 35 who drive nice cars and fly first class to wonderful destinations around the world? Yea, me too. But that's beside the point.

The best way to generate a more highly qualified response is to title your free booklet with a direct benefit to your perfectly targeted customers. Use this formula for your headline: "Free Booklet offers [useful information]." For example: "FREE Booklet shows you how to pack valuables when moving!" The subhead would continue: Call now to get your FREE "Guide to Packing Valuables!" This would produce a ton of the highest-quality leads for a moving company, mostly from people who are planning an immediate move.

When prospects call to say they'd like to get the free guide, the moving company salesperson responds with, "I'd be happy to send it right out. How soon are you moving?" If it's soon, the next question is a natural: "Have you hired a moving company yet?" Instant qualification in under 3 seconds.

Lesson 4:

Show the title of your booklet in the headline of your ad to attract more highly targeted prospects.

Intentionally limiting response to your ad isn't always a bad idea. If your literature and postage is expensive, try this: To increase the value of each response to your offer even further, you may choose to ask for a response by mail that includes a stamped, self addressed envelope. This will wash out the least serious respondents, thereby cutting out pretty much all of the "I saw your toll free number on this-here sheet of paper and decided to call while waiting for my bus!" prospects – saving you on your literature and postage costs.

In consumer offers, if you offer a hefty catalog or something otherwise of good value, you can separate the literature-seekers from more promising serious inquirers by requiring a dollar or two for postage and handling. This will cut your response way down to the really-serious. Viola: more limited response – and only from better prospects. Plus, it's always nice to get some income up front. I know a person who offered a stereo speaker parts catalog and charged $4 for it. He sold more catalogs and had more revenue from selling catalogs than from sales of speaker parts.

Lesson 5: If your literature is expensive, or your market filled with "Consultants" (they never buy, they just want to look at everything...) intentionally limit your response with a tight qualification net or by asking for literature shipping and handling fees.

It's your choice: more respondents who may be less quali-fied, or fewer respondents who are better qualified and more likely to buy. Do you go with the bigger numbers or the better percentages? This depends on your product, dollar amount of sale, lifetime value of a customer (LTV), your offer and your mailing package. We'll discuss this in another article (drop me a self-addressed envelope and I'll send it right out to you.

Please include $2.) See how this works! If I had said, "just leave me an email and I'll send it to you – I'd get inundated with requests. Ugh. This way, I just get the serious folks who'll invest 2 bucks in this information – and also took the time to find an envelope and stamp – no small feat around here...)

I guess the best way to determine what kind of loose or tight qualification net you throw depends on your market, your product, and cost of literature. With a $30 book, if your literature costs you $2 in the mail, and you make $20 on each book sold, you need to sell a book for every 10 mailing packages you send. This is a 10% order rate – not many people achieve that number in the mail, even with a strong direct mail package. But if you're selling a $500,000 printing press – you have a little more room to move.

Lesson 6: When the phone rings, YOU close the sale.

When someone sees your ad and calls your number, your ad worked. Not only that – it worked perfectly. Now it's your turn: it's up to you to sell your product to your customer, not the ad or literature. Selling the product is usually not the primary objective of the ad. You see, It fulfilled its objective – it got someone to call you. Now it's your turn: close the sale.

It's much easier closing a sale on the phone than trying to get someone to buy something from a sheet of paper. You can ask probing questions, see if they're really interested, and find out if they're ready to purchase. I close about 80% of the people who call me up and ask me about my books. All with a money back guarantee, and yes we get returns: we've gotten 3 books back since its first run, the original publication in 1996.

Lesson 7: Save the customers name and address, build a mailing list.

Unless your product is shoddy, the "lifetime value of a customer" or LTV (in case you're in the government and only speak only in acronyms,) is greater than this one single sale.

A person who is happy with your purchase is - at that particular point in time - your most likely prospect. And, they are the cheapest to market to: you already have their name and address, they already know that you supply quality goods at a fair price. You simply need to offer them something else. What else can you offer these most-likely customers?

FREE CATALOGS
OF MAILING LISTS

I WANTED TO KNOW WHAT'S AVAILABLE IN COMPILED LISTS, so I dredged out a few of my direct marketing trade journals from under the mass of papers, old pizza boxes and the few remains of previous lunches on my desk and called all the list vendors in each. Here's what I found out: pizza is only good for three, maybe four days without refrigeration, but the pepperoni still remains tasty for up to a week. Also:

Edith Roman (800-223-2194; www.edithroman.com) publishes an excellent glossy 95 page catalog of both consumer and business response and compiled lists. Lists are alphabetically arranged, also shown by S.I.C. code and geographic breakouts, and counts are included for each list. You can easily find lists of almost any industry: 27,827 stone clay glass and concrete products manufacturers, or any niche: 2,822 ophthalmic goods wholesalers, 2,711 ventilating systems cleaners, 3,086 tattoo parlors. Their catalog is easy to use for both the experienced and others, with a logical layout and explanation of how to use each section. Perfect bound, 8-1/2" x 11".

Dunhill International List Company (800-DUNHILL; www.dunhills.com) publishes an easy to use 77 page 8-1/2" x 11" catalog on bleached newsprint. Dunhill offers specialty lists shown in alphabetized sequence such as 25,921 foundations with officers, 811,000 health insurance agents, and 2,825 single parent organizations; as well as master files of, for example, 2,225,214 women investors, or 588,482 lawyers. They also break out lists by alpha and SIC. As expected, you can get businesses or business executives by state, income, title, type of firm; and attorneys or medical doctors by specialty.

American Business Information (800-555-5335, 402-592-9000; www.infoUSA.com), the firm that went about buying up almost every list company that would sell just a few years ago, offers 11 million businesses by yellow page heading, number of employees, SIC, Sales volume, phone number, credit rating code.. They also offer 195 million consumers by age, estimated income, home value, and other selects. Their 72 page, 8-1/2" x 11" catalog is easy to use and like some of the other catalogs offers a few speciality lists like 12 million executives by ethnic surname, 3 million fax numbers, 663,000 work-at-home businesses, 3 million businesses in affluent neighborhoods to name a few. They also offer lists by SIC, some pretty darn esoteric like 1,068 beverage dispensing equipment wholesalers and 403 bronze table manufacturers. They offer free counts if you call them. When I called and gave them my phone number, they gave me my mailing address and asked if it was still correct.

Acxiom/Direct Media (203-532-1000) had the most pages of advertising in the trade magazines, so I called them. But their 48 page spiral bound catalog paled by comparison to the ease of use of other list catalogs. Their book, mostly response lists, was separated into Business and Consumer sections, showing 30 lists to a page. Only the list name was shown which was sometimes confusing (ie. "Extensis" or "Jasune,") and sometimes not ("Eddie Bauer Baby Furniture") along with the Acxiom customer service rep and sales rep name and phone number. All lists shown in this 8-1/2" x 11" book were managed by Acxiom.

American List Council (800-403-1870; www.amlist.com) sent a 60 page, 8-1/2" x 11" catalog broken down into segments containing consumer lists, business lists, lists by S.I.C. and their proprietary response lists - which included some weird ones such as a master file of ailment sufferers, a few of which I wouldn't want over my house: 537,458 gastritis sufferers, 404,990 bladder control/incontinence sufferers and 790,470 ladies with yeast infections, ouch - that's just gotta hurt. As most of the other major list vendors, they also handle lists for some of the larger mail order houses: 1,337,167 L.L. Bean Buyers M.O.B., 2,695,137 Spiegel M.O.B., and

4,856,781 Victoria's Secret M.O.B.; and some of the larger magazine subscription lists such as 925,243 PC Magazines Subscribers. The catalog is nicely presented and easy to use.

Hugo Dunhill Mailing Lists, Inc. (888-274-5735; www. hdml.com) puts together a well-designed and extremely information-intense catalog of lots and lots of lists. Arranged alphabetically then referenced in S.I.C. order, the Hugo Dunhill catalog goes deep into some wells that are dry in other list house's catalogs. Along with the traditional: 108,472 accounting firms, you can get tax preparers broken down by specialty: 144 associations, 4,305 attorneys, 558 bankers, 25,478 CPAs and so forth. You can also get some esoteric lists: 129 Daughters of the Nile; or a selection of Church Societies (women's) selected by denomination: Methodist Women's Church, Lutheran Church Women's Clubs, or even 84,092 churches with video equipment. Pretty much if you can name it, you can get a list of all the people in it. If you can't name it, call Hugo and speak to him like I did - he's a lot of help in a short amount of time.

Dun and Bradstreet (973-605-6457; www.dnb.com) is one of the granddaddies of the list industry and they warehouse a master file of almost everything and on everybody. They have a full resource file on your credit even if you don't want them to have it. That credit information is available in a list, even if you don't want your competitors to get it. You can also get a CD-ROM with 11 million businesses on it - so you can analyze and manipulate your own data, then pay for only the list of names or businesses you use. Their 48-page catalog is organized by S.I.C.

Compiled lists are a common source of names and records that have been gathered, collected, and entered into a database. Most commonly the names may have been acquired through public records such as vehicle owner registrations or high school teachers; or through directories, such as a directory of plant maintenance engineers. One of the most common sources of information for compiled lists are from yellow page headings: the names are gathered from all the phone books across the U.S. Examples would be all the luggage dealers in the United States, or all the plumbing supply dealers.

Compiled information - like fish - gets old rather quickly and doesn't age particularly well.

Just a note in passing: on the other side of the list industry there are response lists. These are lists of names of people who have responded to offers, most likely inquired or bought something from a catalog or space ad. Response lists are measured by different criteria: how RECENT the names are, how FREQUENTLY they purchase through the mail, and how much MONEY they've spent on a purchase. Names and lists can also be targeted with others who may have made purchases of similar items or are responsive to offers from certain industries. Logic applies: if you are selling a new type of fishing rod, buy a response list from a fishing catalog or a fishing magazine. Response lists are best when they are available for your target market and you are making a direct-selling offer of retail products. Purchase compiled lists to reach your target market when response lists aren't available.

Between response and compiled lists, you can get almost anything you'd like in a list. If you would like to mail to only the people who make the little tiny screws that fit in your eyeglasses, there's a list out there, somewhere, with just the names of those folks on it. It may be a short list, but it's available.

The list catalogs mentioned - and the scores of list catalogs I didn't mention - all have their own ease of use and level of service they provide to their customers. Between the different list houses there are also significant differences in pricing, return policies, and freshness of lists and names. Some vendors clean their lists more frequently. Some offer hot name files that are one month old; some offer hot name files that are 6 months old - you never know until you ask.

Different vendors offer different service levels, too. Some give good marketing advice, others, well... you know. Each list house has its own counts and numbers for different selections, and each treats merged data in different ways. Most list houses have their own particular specialty - so it pays to shop around. My advice: call around and talk to each list house - see who you feel comfortable with. I'll make you this guarantee: the more questions you ask up front, the more response you'll get when you mail.

When you need a great mailing list, just dig. These catalogs - and this article - are just the tip of the iceberg.

PROMOTIONAL MARKETING

Every marketing plan starts the same way: define your audience. Only after you have defined your audience can you figure out the best way to reach them.

Different audiences require different media and campaigns to reach them most effectively and efficiently. Anyone can create an advertising plan - it's easy to spend money. Only a few can create a media plan that is low in cost and produces a good number of higher quality leads that convert into sales. We'll take a look at some different types of promotional media, and discuss the pros and cons of effectively reaching a target audience through each.

We'll also define several types of audience characteristics, but first we'll define marketing. I'll keep it short, just five words if you count the "a". Marketing is "selling to a defined audience." When you offer your goods and services to anyone, that's sales. When you narrow down your offer and present it to your most likely prospects, that's marketing. The benefit of precision in marketing is lower costs by delivering your message (advertising/PR) only to higher quality prospects who are most likely to buy. You spend less initially and, additionally, have less wasted advertising expense.

The cost of reaching people with your advertising message can be defined in terms of CPM, or cost per thousand. You can figure out the cost to reach 1,000 readers of a magazine by dividing the magazine circulation by the cost of the ad. If a full-page, black and white ad costs $2,000, and the magazine reaches 50,000 people, the CPM is $25 - it costs $25 to reach 1,000 people in that magazine. The CPM for each magazine can also be found in a reference book like Oxbridge Communications' Directory of Magazines.

CPM can also be applied to other media, like radio or television; these figures are the language of salespeople in those industries. CPM can also be applied to direct mail - where you'll find it's quite high, from $400 to $500 to reach 1,000 people. But, by using direct mail, you can deliver a longer, more powerful message to a more precisely selected audience.

Perhaps more important are the terms CPI (Cost Per Inquiry) and CPO (Cost Per Order). CPO is the one that really matters. The CPO is the make-or-break number for your business. If your cost per order exceeds your marketing and fulfillment costs, well... better see my other article entitled Plan B, Before Bankruptcy.

How tightly can you pinpoint your target audience? How large is this group (market universe)? How easily can they be reached by the media? The answers will dictate the type of campaign.

Final consideration in promotional media selection is how much each prospect is worth to you if you close the sale. For example, if you are selling printing presses for half a million dollars each, be ready to get a lot of "No thank you's," because you only may sell one press every 18 months to two years. You may only close one prospect in every 20,000 leads, and your CPO may be $8,000. But if you're selling newsletter subscriptions at $39 a pop, you may need to close three of every 100 direct mail pieces you send out (3%).

These are all good marketing examples - to get you thinking about the parameters of your own audiences and marketing expenses. And yes, you have more than one audience. Almost every company and every product has primary, secondary, and tertiary markets. So how do we reach them?

Business-to-business marketing is easy. In most cases this means either trade magazines or direct mail to reach likely prospects, although some industries rely heavily on trade shows, too.

Magazines have good reach in an industry, but almost no depth. You can reach a lot of people, at a lower CPM than in direct mail, but you have a much shorter time to deliver your advertising message, and a much harder time to actually sell a product right from a magazine page. In fact, one of the hardest places in the world to sell a product is from a page in a magazine. You must attract the attention of the reader, then motivate him enough to call. If that's not enough, he must then take out his wallet - no easy feat for a magazine ad. Man, that can be tough.

When creating an ad, write your objective first. If the ad works perfectly, exactly what do you want to happen? Only one percent of the ads I create for clients are hard-hitting, long-copy, direct-selling, call-to-order ads. The objective of 99 percent of the ads I create is not to sell the product. That's right. It's to generate a phone call. You don't sell a $20,000 canning machine from a third-of-a-page ad in a magazine - you create interest and generate a phone call.

The best ways to generate phone calls with ads are 1) to offer something for free; 2) to offer an informational booklet about the product; and 3) to promise the reader a benefit. Very, very high on the list of great headline formulas is "Free Booklet Offers Valuable Information to help you ___." For example, a moving company offers a "Free Booklet on how to pack china for moving." This headline produces a ton of high-quality leads from a qualified market. Another example (more industrial) for a bearing company: "Free Booklet shows how to tell when bearings are starting to wear." OK, so bearings are boring, but this headline will be effective to a precise market: the person who has 5,000 bearings in the machinery at his plant will want this information. The quality of the leads will be very high, and the bearing company won't waste a lot of time stuffing and sending literature to folks who just collect it.

Enough blah, blah, blah. Let's look at some different advertising media - the good, the bad, and the ugly.

MAGAZINES. Overall: good reach, poor depth. Magazines reach both consumer and business-to-business markets. Broad appeal. This is traditionally the way most industrial products are marketed. There are over 10,000 magazines to select from; almost every industry is served by several of its own trade journals.

PROS: May be tightly focused into a particular market or niche. May have the most efficient and cost-effective CPM, CPI, or CPO. The only way to reach some targeted markets efficiently besides direct mail. Circulation figures are general guidelines only. Readership is higher in colder months like January, February, and March, and falls off in summer.

CONS: Magazines aren't read each month by everyone. Most magazines are just scanned by readers. Show issues are poor bets, despite added show distribution. Smaller ads run in the back, some readers never get that far. Competition for readers' attention and response on every page makes your ad easy to miss. The most common response vehicles are the bingo numbers ("Circle number 24 on the reader service card for more information") on reader response cards - and these are the worst quality of leads. While circulation figures remain steady year-round, be aware that readership falls off in the summer as more people spend time outdoors. Almost every inquiry needs to be followed up with a phone call or a direct mail piece - or several. Three-month lead time for ads and press releases in most magazines. Don't believe pass-along readership figures, they're absurd.

RECOMMENDATIONS: Most publishers will give you free space if you create a clever press release. I personally believe a press release is the MOST VALUABLE SINGLE SHEET OF PAPER IN ALL OF MARKETING. A press release can be used to test the effectiveness of a publication to see if it will pull before you place an ad. Never place an ad without negotiating for a press release to be published also.

TRICKS: Additionally, ad position is ALWAYS a negotiated factor. Many magazines discount heavily from their published price list - always ask and negotiate (start by asking for the

12 times rate.) NEVER place three ads in three consecutive issues without running a test ad first - if the first ad fails, you won't have time to cancel the other two. (The publishers don't tell you you have a year to fulfill the 3x rate contract. Place ads 4 months apart - cancel after the first one if it fails.) To create an exceptional headline for your ad, write 100 lines, then go back and pick your best one.

Over 10,000 magazines are published every month - they all want your business. Don't be in a hurry to place an ad - miss one issue and, like streetcars, another comes around shortly. To find any magazine, or to find all the magazines in any particular market, look up the market classification (i.e., photography, banking) in the SRDS Business Magazine Directory, Oxbridge Communications' Directory of Periodicals, Burrelle's Directory of Magazines, or Bacon's Magazine Directory. Consider advertising where competitors consistently run ads.

Direct Mail. You can reach any market, or a selected part of a market, and sell most anything with a good direct mail campaign.

PROS: Creative, interesting mail is well-received. Long copy that is written well can hold a reader's attention and sell products, build loyalty, create brand awareness, sell products, overcome objections, sell products, reach higher-level purchasers, and did I mention sell products?

Easy to test small quantities. Low entrance barriers because of small, intelligent testing quantities. If initial tests are successful, rolling out (mailing to the remainder of the entire list) may be extremely profitable and easy to do: don't change anything, just buy more names and mail the same package. You can get rich by mailing the right offer to the right list.

CONS: Cost to reach a thousand prospects may be quite high at $500 CPM -- and higher. CPM may be too high for some low-cost products. Testing may be expensive. Incorrect selection of a list may completely wipe out any success with a great product, a great package, and a great offer. Testing may be expensive.

RECOMMENDATIONS: Long copy that is boring or dull is thrown out. Unless you are a really incredible writer, keep it short. One overbearingly long letter might make two or three terrific short letters. Include an electrifying letter in every direct mail package, and cram it with benefits. Products have features, benefits are what the customer receives from the feature. For example, a teacup has a handle - that is a feature, the benefit is the customer can hold a hot cup without getting burned.

Lead with your best stuff, your biggest benefit, then expound on that. A short bulleted list of benefits gets high readership. Don't forget to ask the reader to call, I usually do this several times in the letter. Enclose your brochure for credibility and to show features. The secret of direct mail: show the benefits in the letter, sell the call hard, and show features in your brochure.

YELLOW PAGES. Ugh. A necessary evil if you are a retailer. The sales pitch you get from the yellow-page salesman is plagued by double talk and jargon you won't hear anywhere else. But this medium can be one of the most effective advertising sources for selected businesses. Some businesses - like emergency drain cleaning - are completely driven by yellow-page advertising.

PROS: Reaches consumers at an excellent time: when they are ready to shop, or when they need information about products they are about to purchase.

CONS: Expensive. You are quoted monthly rates by sales personnel, but your contract is for a year. Over the years, the marketing gurus at the Old Ma Bell Company (remember those days?) figured out exactly how to cut the book up to extract the maximum amount of money from each client. You gotta admit, they were pretty good at it.

RECOMMENDATIONS: Everyone likes to shop in their own back yard, so orient your listing to have your town or area in the biggest letters possible. I prefer to be listed "in-line" with a "Logo Ad." To see exactly what this is, look up the airlines. This is my recommendation: instead of your logo, place your town name in the logo slot. It's OK to tell the rep that's your logo. Really. (Just don't tell them I said so.) Use short, crisp wording, throwing a wide net to get people to call ("We stock all kinds of____, call for information"; "Large stock of widgets - huge inventory, call for fast, friendly help"). Don't forget, the primary objective is to sell the call. The objective of the call is to have customer come in or buy your service.

RADIO. An effective medium if the listener doesn't have to write anything down. Works well with large events and broad-audience demographics. Most effective when ads are repeated over and over. Stations are priced by their Arbitron ratings, and rates are always negotiable. Stations cater to specific audiences, usually grouped by age. You may be paying for people out of your demographic target group - or your geographic area - especially if you are a retailer.

PROS: If you need a general audience, and have more than one or two locations around town, this medium may be ideal. Radio stations will write your ad and produce it for free. Since it has quick response, it's easy to test. Works well with immediate sales.

CONS: Tough to benchmark, or to predict response. Can be expensive. Small numbers of ads don't test well. Audience must be willing to drive to your location for your product. You pay for reaching everyone in the entire area that can receive the station - if these aren't all potential customers, better rethink this medium. Commercials may need to be obnoxious to be noticed.

RECOMMENDATIONS: Great for selected businesses or products having a broad-base audience that can remember the 10 digits in a phone number or address. Works well with vanity numbers that spell a word (800-FLOWERS). Can work for insurance, disc jockey services, sports events, shows, big (sounding) sales events.

Spots are assigned to run at approximate times like "morning drive" or "midday," each at varying rates. Negotiate for the best times - there's a big difference between 8:30 a.m., when everyone is in their car, and 9:05 a.m. when most are at work. Never buy ROS (run of station), where the station places your spots anywhere they want. "Don't worry, we'll place it where it will work best" isn't a good assurance - it's YOUR money, and YOUR money gone if the ad fails to draw. Radio is IMMEDIATE - virtually ALL your response will come within two or three days of the ad, unless you own a restaurant - where there may be some delay for patrons to schedule. Remember, there is a commercial on right before yours, and another right after yours.

WEB ADVERTISING. No, the Internet isn't going to go away. Yes, it's getting stronger every day. Yes, more and more people are using it. No, most people aren't making money on it. OK, Dell Computers is making a quadrillion dollars a day on it. But don't get your hopes up too much, not just yet anyway.

Although still emerging from its infancy, the web is a good place to supplement your traditional advertising with a longer sales pitch - cleverly disguised as worthwhile information - at your website. While it's possible to drive casual surfers to your site, it's unlikely. Being listed in search engines won't help unless a search brings you up in the top thirty or so spots. Being 300th is the same as being 300,000 as far as most consumers are concerned.

Three possible attractants to your site: 1. links from a billion other sites - or a few strategic ones, such as links from your association or industry magazines; 2. going into every conceivable chat room and blog you can find and, at opportune times only, butting in with "Yes, I agree, but at my site www.nowayjose.com you can see for yourself 45 other ways to..."

The third way is quite good: Paid listings at search engines. This has spawned a new era in advertising and can be quite effective and cost efficient if done correctly. This - out of all ways to advertise - is my favorite. Quite good considering I'm not really a web guy but mostly centered in the old school of print media. Since it's so big, and so intricate - with so many ways to do it, we'll discuss in another article at length.

One day soon this will be bigger than all of us, and OH MY GOD IT IS ALREADY... Therefore, soon it will be taxed heavily by many methods in every corner and crevice by every governmental agency of national, state, and local governments. Better get in now.

PROS: Cutting-edge technology. It pays to stay in the loop; there are new opportunities opening up every day. If you can get people to your site, and if you can keep their attention, you can probably sway them into your arms but not into your hands. Don't count your money just yet. Sales are brisk for on-line auctions, computer paraphernalia, music, books, travel, selected industries, and IPOs, but most - even some really big players - are losing really big money. It's a great way for us as consumers to shop price and to research almost anything. To hit a home run here you're going to need to be really clever, or stay at bat for a long time. But it can be done, and there are now lots of very profitable sites.

CONS: Tough to get people to your site. It's like having a phone number no one knows, or a library with books in no particular order. All your print advertising must have your special URL landing page so you can track it.

RECOMMENDATIONS: Get a good advisor and a quality site based on clear objectives and expectations. Make sure you have a reasonable objective of what you want your site to do. Banner ads can be effective but usually aren't, look-up site profiles on the SRDS Interactive Advertising Source - it shows site-company profiles, visitor hits and pages per week, cost of links and banner ads, and so forth. Bulk email, ugh, can work if crafted correctly, but watch out - don't let the flames burn your butt, er, back end. Search engine ranking and paid ad words are the way to go - and you can get in rather easily and cheaply.

TRADE SHOWS. Each year there are over 10,000 trade shows. They're all listed in the Trade Show Week Data Book; the top 2,000 are shown on their website www.tradeshowweek. com. I've never been sorry I attended a trade show. There is a wealth of knowledge - focused around a particular cause or industry - assembled in one place. You can learn a lot in a short period of time.

Trade shows are excellent ways to get industry information, find resources, receive product feedback, generally explore new ways of marketing face-to-face with both exhibitors and attendees, poke around and find out information, and have fun, too.

PROS: Face-to-face presentation: selling at its best. If you can't close them here, you're at the wrong show or in the wrong business. An opportunity to meet competitors, trade friends, and customers. Can establish and cement yearly friendships.

CONS: While booth space may be cheap, don't forget to factor in the cost of getting a crew there, putting them up, putting up with them all day for three days or so in a 10-foot space, treating them all to nice lunches, and then nicer dinners, and getting them home safely. Don't forget all the work you left sitting on your desk. Don't forget all the work they left sitting on their desks. Get the best booth location you can. Don't spend too much time speaking with each passerby - get a business card and rate them for later follow up, then let them go on their way.

RECOMMENDATIONS: Shows can be expensive, so visit any show first as an attendee before even considering booth space. When you get your own booth, have your two-minute spiel down pat before you go live. Have an objective and a goal for exhibiting. Follow-up is a necessary evil, but the ONLY way to make the show pay off. Can't make it? Consider buying the mailing list of either exhibitors or attendees.

TV. While the national channels like ABC, CBS, and other big-time boys are for the big-time advertisers like Coke and

Reebok, one of the best media buys for the past 10 years has been local cable. If you're shooting for local demographics, cable can be focused to neighborhoods around your storefront (subscriber lists are as small as 10,000 households).

Years ago - when I was a kid - OK, so maybe I wasn't quite a kid, anyhow, we only got three channels clearly. Sure, we received a few fuzzy UHF channels, and if you held the antenna just right, you could get roller derby(!) with the San Francisco Bay Bombers... you see these girls used to come out in tight outfits and roller skates... but that's another story. Today's TV selection (with the cable being wired like a big umbilical cord into our houses giving us another life) offers 50, 80, 100 channels - great for the viewer but much tougher for the advertiser. Great care must be taken to place ads where the audience demographics for the show makes them work. The good news: once you stumble onto the formula, you can run an ad ad nauseam and it will continue to pull well for years.

PROS: Cheap to test. Spots as low as $15 to $20. Commercials can be shot by a local commercial video studio for $350 to $500 for a 30-second spot. You can become famous - albeit just in your own neighborhood. You can be effective in a 30-second ad, since it's auditory and visual, and the demographics can be tailored for your store or shop.

CONS: Multitude of channels makes selection of where to place an ad very difficult at best, a nightmare at worst. Reps who sell ad time may not know where your ad will work best - only where they have time available, or which shows or time slots they have been asked to push by the station management.

RECOMMENDATIONS: Negotiate hard for ad time and extra spots (free). NEVER take ROS - run of station - where the station puts your ad in where they like (longer running ad schedules and larger clients get the best spots). Track response closely.

CARD DECKS. Sure, you get them in the mail and skim through them - sometimes. Why would someone in their right mind look through a bunch of ads? I don't know either. Card decks range up to 64 cards in a pack and are mailed to specific lists. Many card decks are sent by magazines to their subscriber list. Mailings are usually 100,000; advertisers can often mail to half the deck to test or split the run with two different offers.

PROS: Card decks are so effective for some companies that they market solely through this medium. Decks are mailed on a regular basis but usually less frequently than a magazine - on average four times a year.

CONS: Expensive to test. Your card can get lost in the pack. Since there are so many decks marketed, if the one you purchase lands with two or three others on the same day, there's a good likelihood it will get tossed out.

RECOMMENDATIONS: Study the deck you are interested in - don't be in a hurry to purchase. Look for other similar offers - those that have been run time after time (ask the rep how long and how frequently they've been running). All decks are initially priced at $2,400 to $3,500 per card, full run. This price is for tourists - most are actually sold at $1,400 to $1,700 per card, or less. A few fetch $2,400 consistently. Some decks can be bought for $700 - $800 per card. Negotiate price!

Your card's position in the deck DOES matter, always negotiate EXACT position. Don't settle for "We'll give you good position" - their idea of good position (first half of deck) and your idea of good position (in the first five cards) won't show up except in hindsight and in missed orders. Too late then, isn't it? Then you'll get experience - which is what you get when you don't make any money.

Use the second side of your card for sales copy - it's a waste of valuable ad space to use it as a name and address side. The headline accounts for 90% of your readership - write a great one. Use the Jeff Dobkin 100 to 1 Rule: write 100 headlines, go back and pick the very best one.

NEWSPAPERS. One of the more immediate advertising venues. Lead time for an ad is just a day or two so testing is easy and fast. Different sections make it easy to select more targeted readers, but dilute general offers because no one can read all the papers every day.

PROS: Selectivity in areas served - hometown or across the country. Different sections draw different readership so you can target your ad to your market. Newspapers work for a large variety of offers: sales, products, shops, retailers, service organizations. Wide selection - just in my own neighborhood there are 30 newspapers to choose from.

CONS: Too many papers dilute the market. Bigger ads can blow out your small ad. Your ad can get lost in the clutter in larger papers (metro). Big run papers can be expensive for small advertisers (large advertisers get huge discounts for running volume lineage). Your ad may be grouped with competitors.

RECOMMENDATIONS: Testing is the way to go. Some of my clients have had good success with the TV Listings section, some with the Business section. Negotiate good placement in the paper and good placement on the page. Sundays may not be as good as weekdays for some - too much paper! Wednesday is coupon day and high female readership. Don't forget local weeklies and classifieds. Local papers are much cheaper than larger metropolitan papers and provide better demographics for single retail stores. Don't forget to send press releases to test the publication before you contract for an ad.

Don't forget other advertising mediums such as advertising specialties, small imprinted items with your name on them; FSI's, free standing inserts usually consisting of four-color coupons found in the Sunday papers (a half-page has a CPM as little as $2.40); coupon mailers that arrive at your home such as Val-Pak or Ad Art; bus and bench advertising; outdoor billboards; movie and theater advertising; school newspapers and yearbooks; outdoor advertising by aerial (skywriting and airplane billboard [$325/hr.], hot air balloons, and blimp advertising); inflatables (for example, a 35' King Kong is

$500/day); bus bench/ bus shelter; truck/mobile advertising; taxi; telephone kiosk; and transit advertising.

Hey, while you're at it don't forget airport advertising, and high school/college campus advertising, plus advertising in hotels, in-flight, in-store, shopping mall, and sports/fitness/ leisure facility, stadium/arena/sports team advertising, truck and truckstop advertising, and event marketing.

Other sources of unconventional advertising are Entertainment coupon books, supermarket entrance advertising (community bulletin boards), package - insert programs from almost every type of merchandiser and direct mailer, Internet ads and websites, orchestra program books (great for upscale audiences), professional and local theater program books, local team sponsorships, college sports programs, motor-racing events programs, town festival programs, messages on hold, ATM messages, supermarket register tape programs, and synagogue and church bulletins and yearbooks - to name a few. Wow. It's enough to make you dizzy.

Whatever you do, don't forget to track response. When working with any print media, send press releases. Always negotiate price and position. Call anytime (610-642-1000) if you have questions or get stuck.

GETTING CUSTOMERS THROUGH DIRECT MARKETING

Get new customers. Now keep them, by making sure they stay satisfied and happy. All with low-cost, tested direct marketing methods. Sound good? Here's how.

Direct marketing is a low cost way of reaching-in with your message and piercing that gruff exterior customer shell and finding your way into their hearts, minds... and wallets. It doesn't matter whether you get all of your business from a half-dozen large accounts right in your own neighborhood, or if you are marketing a new product to millions of folks worldwide.

Major Uses of Direct Marketing Campaigns

Direct marketing can be the most effective way to get leads and deliver hot prospects. It's also used to sell to customers directly, without further human intervention. As an added bonus, it's easy and cheap to use these same direct marketing methods to retain current customers and keep them happy. I say CRM, customer retention management, but what crap - a new term pinned on something we've been doing for years - keeping customers happy.

Here's an example. I was once called in to analyze the marketing program of a large insurance company. I found out they lost about a third of their customers every two years. Further analysis showed me why.

"I know what your customer received from you in your last correspondence with them," I said with a smile. They looked at me, puzzled at how I would know. I continued, "It was a bill." Everyone smiled and nodded. I was right. Now the bad news: after two years of bills, and not one "Thank you for your business!" letter, most people just drifted off to another provider. For the price of sending two letters each year specifically to thank customers, I figured they could boost their customer retention rate by 75%. You can too. Same low cost: 82¢ a year.

Direct Mail: Still the lowest cost marketing tool

Despite the continual rising costs of postage, direct marketing is still a great value. It's the lowest-cost type of marketing because of its precision and accuracy. With direct mail you can send a message to a specific target audience without a lot of wasted expense. For example, you can mail just 100 letters to a list of your 100 best prospects. This simple project is one of the most effective direct marketing campaigns I can think of, and I recommend this to any business. Over the next 6 months, mail a letter to your 100 best prospects each month and it actually is the single most effective campaign, ever. Any arguments?

So, for the cost of a single letter to 100 prospects, all of $37 in postage plus a couple hundred sheets of paper, you can pierce the corporate veil. You can, with a surety of 95% or better, get a piece of paper with your own message, and in fact your own personal signature on it, to land on the desk of almost anyone. This list includes presidents of large corporations, government officials, HR directors, chain store buyers, even the person who buys products for L.L. Bean or the Brookstone Catalog. Whomever. How great is that? How effective is that? I don't think you can do any better than that with any other marketing method.

So here's one of my best marketing tips: Do it now. Write several tight, great letters and mail them to your 100 best prospects over the next several months. Send a copy to me, too. I'll respond and give you my thoughts, I promise.

Types of Direct Marketing

The primary route for direct marketing is the mail and for good reason: you can aim a single piece of marketing material directly at your absolute best target with the precision of a sharpshooter. The ammunition you use? It can be a post card, self mailer, brochure, flyer, letter — all with or without an envelope. Each has its place in the marketing mix. Let's take a look, along with the view through scope you're using: the mailing list of possible targets.

Post cards —

Post cards rock because they have exceptionally high readership - by the time your recipient gets it in his or her hand... it's... it's... already read. Other advantages: Easy to address, cheaper to mail than letters and cheap to print, too. There are lots of great specialty post card printers; post cards can be printed in 4 colors and purchased for about $400 for 5,000. Just look around for great prices. I also like post cards printed in just one or two colors. Well thought-out cards can be striking in copy and graphics even if your budget is limited to printing cards in just one color.

Post cards work best as lead generation devices, especially for products that people are already familiar with. Cons: You can't tell a long story, or offer a consultative selling proposition. Also, post cards are always impersonal and suffer from a reader's short attention span - if you don't capture the reader's attention in the first 3 seconds, the card gets tossed. In a big office there is a danger that the card may be thrown away early by a mail screener. For additional information on post cards, see my article, "Marketing with Post Cards" elsewhere at this site, or at www.dobkin.com.

Recommendation: Make your post cards work hard by generating a phone call to you. Use a strong headline - grab attention fast! Flaunt your biggest benefit to immediately capture the interest of your audience. This is no place to be subtle. Since there's little room for long sales copy, write copy to generate a phone call from a qualified prospect instead of trying to actually sell your product directly from the card. Just flush out the interested, offer to send them a longer (harder-selling) package if oh, they would just pick up the phone and call now. Print your phone number in a large, bold typeface.

Self Mailer —

These can take on any of thousands of forms, shapes and folds; from a simple trifold to a 5-color, box-cut, pre-scored, diecut 12-fold brochure with a handy self-addressed, already filled out with the customer's name reply card attached. Self-mailers allow you to show the most creativity and personality. Cons: Very short runs are impractical for complex pieces or 4 color. They usually aren't personal and are almost never warm and fuzzy.

Recommendation: Use striking graphics and set a unique tone. Ask yourself, "If he receives this in the mail again in 4 months, will he remember he received it before?" If you answered no, go back and redesign the piece to make it a more memorable. Make your piece hard-selling - remember if they didn't call, your piece failed. The creative use of one or two colors work just fine and can save on printing costs.

Letter —

As an effective marketing tool, this is my own personal favorite. With a well-written and well-designed letter, you can generate a lead, or actually make a person pick up the phone and call to place an order. What more could you ask for from a few sheets of paper? Oh, yeah - you can do that too: endear someone, build loyalty, and convince them they are the most important customer in the world. Yes, with a letter - just a sheet or two of paper. Cons: If you can't write a tight, memorable letter, you can sink like a stone without a ripple.

Take your time writing. It may take you a few weeks to write a great one page letter - but that's OK. I have clients call me up all the time and say they just can't come up with a letter that is as good as one of mine. I ask how long they worked on it, and they say "Oh, about half an hour." I tell them to go back and put in the other 8 hours. It still takes me 8 to 10 hours to write a tight, one-page letter.

Recommendation: Spend some time writing and refining and editing your letter. The best campaign I've ever written (which can be found in my book, Uncommon Marketing Techniques) is a series of letters, each sent about a month apart, to a list of a handful of my best, tightly-qualified prospects. Feel free to use these letters for your own personal campaign... once you buy my book, of course. Or download them elsewhere on this site for just $20.

- Letter and Brochure —

An envelope containing a letter and a brochure is the workhorse of the direct mail industry. There's a reason: this format works well for a multitude of offers. The letter sells, and the brochure tells. Design the letter to sell the benefits and generate the phone call. Design the brochure to add credibility to the letter. It's one thing to say in a letter "Our Olympic size pool with swim-up bar is breathtaking." It's another to show it in a 12" x 18" photo pull-out. Cons: This format is overused, making it difficult to leave a unique impression.

Recommendation: This is the easiest format to use in mailings, and the most successful format for most mailers. I recommend this format for both large and small firms. You are working with the same 2 sheets of paper as everyone else: get creative. Get noticed. And get a phone call - which should the the objective both sheets are written to.

Successful Mailings

There are several common elements that pertain to anything you send in the mail. First: Design each piece to a specific objective. What are you actually trying to do with this piece? If the piece works perfectly as planned, what exactly will happen in the very next step? Generate a sale? Generate a lead? Generate a phone call? Secure an order? Make someone feel good about you and your firm? Set up a prospect to receive your phone call? Create an impression the recipient won't forget? Whatever it is, write it down first, then draft each each word, each piece of your mailing package to fulfill your objective. This gives you additional clarity when writing.

I've seen more direct mail response killed by the author writing to the wrong objective. And here's the most common killer: Trying to sell a product from the page, instead of trying to generate a phone call and a qualified lead. Beware of this trap. If your product or service needs more than 200 words to sell it successfully, go for the lead generation package. However, if you can write a long and well-focused direct mail package, it is possible to sell products or services.

Creating The Letter

First, create a striking headline -

Like an ad or press release your letter has a headline: it's your opening sentence. In fact, your opening sentence should also be your whole first paragraph. Yes - your whole first paragraph should be just a single sentence, two at most.

Just like in an ad, the first line of your letter never sells anything. The objective of the first line is to arouse interest, otherwise your package faces an early death - by trash can.

I recommend you use the Jeff Dobkin 100 to 1 rule (from an article in my book, Uncommon Marketing Techniques, called, appropriately, The 100 to 1 Rule): write 100 headlines, then go back and pick out your best one. Hey, I didn't say you'd like it, I just said it would be effective at helping you to create a great headline.

Still stuck? Throw your biggest few benefits into the headline; here's the headline formula: "New product offers benefit, benefit, benefit!" Example: "New sprinkler waters your lawn more thoroughly yet saves water, reaches a larger area, and turns itself off when finished."

Another formula for creating a great headline, offer something for FREE, preferably free information: "FREE BOOKLET shows you how to benefit, benefit, benefit!" "FREE BOOKLET shows you how to repair your leaky roof, stop downspouts from clogging, and keep leaves from accumulating in wet areas."

Let readers express early interest by calling you and asking for your booklet. When the phone rings the last thing you do is ask for their name and address to send the booklet. First, you strike up a dialog. Qualify them as a prospect, suspect, or someone with a phone in their bathroom and no magazines. Remember, when the phone rings, the letter or mailer worked. Now it's your turn. Design tip: whenever you use the word FREE in a letter or brochure, make sure it's in all capital letters.

Expound on your biggest benefit -

Don't hold back: flaunt your biggest and best stuff first. If you wait until the 6th page to show the FREE Chevrolet Corvette that comes FREE with every policy, your readers will be long gone by page two.

In direct mail you fire off your biggest guns up front! Be succinct and fast paced, especially in the first page of your letter. Reason: with the first page of copy, there is no commitment to continue reading. If your letter is only so-so, it'll be so-long: a short history lesson you tried to teach by the end of the first page. Keep the reader moving along, especially in the early part of the letter.

If your letter is great until the 5th page, the reader is hooked by that time. He's interested, and by page 5 the reader has already made a commitment to continue reading. So at all costs, keep your reader reading through the first half of your package. The longer he's in your package, the better your opportunity to sell him something.

Here's a third rule: Keep it short. It's much better to say too little and have the reader call for more information, than to spill your guts out all over his desk and have him throw the package away before finishing.

Enough rules. If you want more rules, get married. Just kidding. I married a wonderful woman... and that's not just my opinion, it's her's.

Letter design -

So... let's see... oh, yes - we were writing about our biggest benefit and how wonderful our product or service is, how much they'll enjoy it. If you're selling via a direct offer, remind them, they could have it all... ohhhhhh, if they'd just send you only $29.95, but better hurry - supplies are limited! Spend a paragraph or two expounding your biggest benefit. Keep paragraphs short - 7 lines maximum. Vary paragraph length.

Create a bulleted list of benefits and place that list right in the middle of your page. Bulleted lists have exceptionally high readership and act to break up the copy and make the letter visually attractive and appear easy to read.

If the objective of your letter is lead generation, offer a "FREE booklet of worthwhile information," to generate a phone call. Can you come up with a booklet title that is so entrancing your readers MUST have it? Use it here. By using a "FREE booklet" technique with a powerful must-have title, your letter can now be much shorter. Interested parties will go for the free booklet.

If your product or service is a consultive-type sell - if your product, service or selling proposition needs a long explanation; or if you're selling something high priced, you'll need to send a longer letter. But don't let your message - and offer - get lost in the clutter. Remember, one overly long sales letter gets thrown out, three short letters saying the same thing all get read.

Call me crazy but I like to ask for a phone call several times in the letter, and in the last paragraph in the body copy I generally place my phone number right in the copy, even though it's in the letterhead. It's a subtle suggestion to call again.

Sign legibly. While you may scribble your signature on checks, direct mail readers want to be able to see it's really you - so your signature becomes a graphic hook: make sure they can read it.

Finally, restate your most powerful argument for calling or ordering in the PS. Keep it short and sweet - and put your phone number in the PS again, even though you may have it other places.

The Brochure

Show the benefits of what you're selling (the great things that happen to the reader if he buys and uses your products) in the letter, and show the features (physical points of what your service or the product has) in the brochure.

Of course, being an old direct marketing guy, I always like to place a few of our biggest benefits in the brochure, too. Here's why: Brochures usually need to be designed to be a stand-alone piece - so they can be mailed, left at a prospect's office or handed out during a show. As such, I recommend you always show your top three or four benefits in the brochure.

The brochure can be one, two or four colors. If there's only room in the budget for one color - call it a "Data Sheet"; they work just fine in black and white. Either way, a good design implies that the reader will receive a well-designed product. I firmly believe great design negates the necessity of four color.

Please note: Never, ever stick a brochure in an envelope and call it a direct mail campaign. Always, always include a letter. For the additional cent and a half for the sheet of paper that your letter costs to include, it's cheap insurance and can double, triple, quadruple - or more - the response you receive.

The Envelope

My preference is to design everything in my mailing package for one fold (5-1/2" x 8-1/2") which - is my own personal favorite, to be mailed in a 6" x 9" envelope. More traditionally letters and brochures are designed to be folded in thirds to fit into a more standards number 10 envelope (9" x 4"). Ugh.

Teaser on the envelope? My favorite: "Gift Certificate Enclosed!" Your certificate can be good for your informational booklet, ("A $7.95 value, sent to you FREE with the this Free Gift Certificate.) Gift certificates are cheap to print, ship flat, have no cost until redemption, can be offered for excess material you'd like to get rid of.

Don't like teaser copy? Here's another cheap trick: just type your name and business address (no business name) on the envelope corner, then hand write or image the name and address directly on the envelope (no labels) and people will think it's a personal letter from you. You'll enjoy higher-than-normal opening rates.

Mailing Lists

Of all the places to err, the selection of the wrong mailing list is the worst. If you buy the wrong list, your mailing produces, umm... nothing. It's like trying to sell Chevy hubcaps to Ford station wagon owners.

The best list you can mail to is your own house list of your own prospects and customers. Did I make that clear enough? Start gathering names right now.

If you can figure out the common elements that make your customers unique, you can specify those characteristics in a mailing list. Purchase mailing lists from brokers (found in the phone book), or better yet get a copy of Target Marketing Magazine (215-238-5270; www.targetonline.com), and you'll find dozens of brokers to call and harass, er... ask questions to.

There's usually a 5,000 name minimum for buying or renting mailing list names. This doesn't mean you have to mail to 5,000 names, but you may have to buy this amount.

There just isn't room to do justice for list selection criteria in this article, so here's where to go for more information. Mailing lists are the critical element in direct marketing campaigns, and you can find selection criteria at my web site (www.dob-kin.com) and also... check out my books at a library, they'll order them for you - just ask: How To Market A Product For Under $500, and Uncommon Marketing Techniques.

I'd be happy to send you 3 articles I've written on mailing lists: "12 Questions To Ask a List Broker," "FREE Catalogs of Mailing Lists," and "How To Buy a Great Mailing List." The cost is $7 and please include a large stamped (5 oz. = $1.29 postage) envelope. Credit card orders - just give me a call: 610-642-1000. Criteria for selecting a mailing list varies with what you are selling, what you are offering, the market, and how tightly you can define your targets - who your most likely customers are.

Low cost testing

Any major mailing first goes through a small-mailing test-ing stage. This is where you mail smaller quantities to figure out if mailing to the entire list will be profitable. While you can mail just 100 letters to a house list and be profitable, the results from this small of a mailing to a rented list won't be reliable.

If you're a real small firm, mail 500 pieces to test the results. The more you mail, the greater the accuracy of your prediction of the success you'll have with your next mailing to the same list. At around 1,000 pieces you can start to get a real feel for the success of your list and package.

The biggest benefit of direct mail is that once your mailing package is successful and profitable from smaller test mail-ings, you can start ramping-up to larger and larger mailings using the exact same package to the same list. If you do this correctly, you'll find you'll keep getting the same results. I know a lot of people who have gotten very rich from this method of marketing.

Here's a handy tip: If you're selling a product directly from your direct mail package, start out by doing the math backwards. Figure out what percentage of people need to purchase your product to cover the cost of the mailing. Figure your mailing costs at 50¢ per package. (This cost comes down with larger mailings.)

For example: If you mail to 1000 people, you'll need to cover $500 in mailing expense, then your cost of fulfillment (product cost plus shipping), plus some profit left over for you to call your mailing a success. If you need more than a 1-1/2% to 2% response to cover your costs - and profit - to produce a successful mailing, better rethink. If your product sells for $25 and your profit is $10 each after shipping, you need to sell 50 units to cover the cost of postage and break even. That's a 5% response - unrealistically high.

Most direct-response rates for direct sales are under 2%, and most - well under. But by giving away a FREE booklet with an awesome, must-have title, your response can be as high as 25%. But your hard-selling, secondary package to this more qualified list must be able to draw enough response to cover all costs. Looking at these figures you can see why products that sell for less than about $50 don't work in solo direct mailing. Even at $50 list, with a profit of $25 per sale, you need to sell 20 units per thousand to break even - a 2% order rate.

These numbers show you why your list selection is so important: if you can find a highly focused group of people (or market segment) that all want your product and are most likely - and are willing - to order from your mailer you might just find success.

Sidebar

Looking at all your advertising options? Direct marketing is the lowest cost, and most precise of all advertising venues because it offers the least amount of wasted advertising expense. And it's fully testable - you never have to lose big money if you just test small quantities. But - and like my aunt Martha, this is a big butt - you need to have a highly qualified list to mail to.

Direct marketing is excellent for both generating leads and closing sales. A small, effective direct mail campaign is as easy as placing a few hundred letters in the mail to your best prospects, which is one of my most highly recommended campaigns. I can't imagine anyone I'd rather write to than a well-focused list of my best prospects. Can you? There should be room in every business marketing budget for some type of direct mail campaign.

THINKING ABOUT GOING ON-LINE? INSURANCE. AND MAILING LISTS.

Now that the Internet has come and gone... What? What was that? The Internet is still here? Well, excuse me. I didn't know it was still up and running. And who's really running the damn thing, anyhow.

I see more stuff about the Internet and how people are making money, how people aren't making money, how it's going to take over the insurance industry, how it's going to take over the airline ticket industry, and, and how it's going to take over the world... and it just ain't happening, is it?

It didn't really replace your daily newspaper, did it? No, it didn't. It didn't replace all those magazines you get, did it? No, I didn't think so. It didn't even replace those special magazines you get in the brown wrapper. Ha, caught you! You thought no one knew about them - but I can buy your name on more than one mailing list. The Internet does have lots of porn sites, though, er, at least that's what friends tell me.

Here's a funny story - I'll be brief. When I first got connected to the Internet and was just, umm, exploring, and I must have, umm, accidentally typed in xxx, and then my elbow must have hit the return key because suddenly there were pictures of naked ladies right up there on my CRT. Wow, I thought to myself, I don't get that channel at home...

So, a few minutes later when naked women became old hat... and... and... ok, you got me. So a few hours later while I was still there searching for the free sites and pictures of more naked women doing all kinds of things I haven't seen since college, in black and white, on 8mm, without sound —to let you know how old I really am — I decided it's too much fun, it must be illegal, and besides, maybe I'd just better get back to work.

So, just then the UPS guy came bounding up the stairs - a prerequisite to getting to my office, so I quickly hit the close box to get the lovely lasses off my large, 22", you-can-get-a-sunburn-from-sitting-too-close monitor, when I made my first amazing discovery about the Internet: the pop-up window.

Now frantically closing pop-up after pop-up of evidently famous women (in some circles) with some of the largest, and um well, anyhow then there was me and the UPS guy staring at the screen of pop-up after pop-up of women who are evidently hornier than I've ever been - even through my chronically hormonally imbalanced days of college.

"So," he said with a smile after a few seconds, "I guess you're not getting much work done these days?" Big grin on his face. It was pretty embarrassing. Got him back, though. The next day I shipped 400 pounds of books to myself at my home address. Then I shipped them back. The smart ass. You've never seen a UPS man as mad as when you make him take 400 pounds of books down a flight of stairs, unless it's when he has to carry them back up the next day. I think he's still a little pissed at me for that; I see a lot of my deliveries that look like the one from the beginning sequence of Ace Ventura, Pet Detective.

It's been a few years since I've seen that wild group of Internet women. Where the heck were all those girls when I was single and dating? I couldn't even get to first base after dating a lady for months. And that was nice dinner after nice dinner... if you like Greek diner food. Heck, I even let them order dessert for a chance at second base. Well at least some of them. Not that I'm here to complain. I'm here to help you sell insurance. No, I take that back. I'm here to help you make the phone ring. It's up to you to sell insurance.

But not just yet. There's the PS to the story. Over the next several months I learned my second big lesson about the Internet: spam from porn sites, where I embarrassed myself again by opening an email from "You remember me, Cindy?" - in front of my secretary. In my defense, I have to say I didn't know anyone could walk around without falling over forward if they were that big. And I guess she just wore slip-on shoes because tying a pair of sneaks was just completely out of the question.

OK, let's get back to work. Is the Internet a good place to market insurance? No. Next question.

Should you have a web presence? Yes. Hey, it's 2008. You should have a face in the electronic community. Let's take a practical look at how you can and can't use a web site.

Let me first say that if you are a web merchant selling insurance, this article isn't for you. Sure, there are success-ful insurance merchants that sell on-line, but that's a whole other industry. This article is written for the agents in the trenches: on the front lines at retail storefronts, and at small and medium size offices selling life, casualty, and health (and related insurance products) to homeowners, business own-ers, and sometimes anyone that will stand still long enough to listen to their pitch.

Rule 1.

Define the objective of your website. Nothing beats poor site architecture and lousy copy... except having no apparent reason that you have a site at all. Let's take a look at some web site objectives.

To inform your customers and prospects about your prod-ucts.

After your welcome page, you direct visitors to the laundry list of the many types of coverage you can acquire for them. This acts as a memory jogger, and shows customers you are a very full service agency that can handle all their insurance needs. Each page on your site then encourages visitors to call you for a quick quote, with questions, or for more information.

To build credibility.

Put your best foot forward with rich, lavish photos of yourself and staff, copy that exudes your confidence that you can handle any business - or business questions - they throw your way. Include a client list and testimonials, then encourage visitors to call you for a fast and friendly quote, with questions, with service needs, or for more information.

To provide information.

Informational sites build credibility in another way - by establishing you as an expert in the field. This kind of site works well with articles, white papers, links, reference resources, useful statistics, and other pertinent industry information that makes you 'da man, and entices viewers to keep coming back. Each page on your site then encourages visitors to call you for a quick quote, with questions, or for more information.

To blow off clients you don't want to speak with.

Just ask Sprint, Verizon, AT&T, MCI or any of the big phone companies a question and what do you get? 20 Minutes on-hold while they repeatedly tell you to go to their website. It's wonderful for them: they don't have to spend the 30 seconds answering your questions with a live person when they can send you somewhere else and have you spend 3 hours trying to look it up. You can do this too, to clients you don't like or no longer need.

Using your web site instead of your brochure.

While your brochure can be left behind to sit on someone's desk, can be read in the bathroom, or used in the living room or office as a great coaster, your website can't. So while a website doesn't replace your brochure in all its functions, it can give you instant credibility, and verification of your firm's presence to someone you are speaking with on the phone.

While they're on the phone with you, they can look up your site in real time and you can establish a comfort zone with them: that you are a legitimate organization. It's just one more link in the credibility chain. Then your site encourages visitors to call you for a fast and friendly quote, with questions, or for more information.

Sales.

Notice I placed sales well down on the list. There's a reason: your web site is the last place to try to make a sale. Unless your site is set up specifically to generate a sale from the opening page, and continues with this objective to the last "Thank you for your order" on its order form, forgedaboudit. Your site should be pointing at the phone to generate a phone call. Hey, learn to take the order: spend the three minutes on the phone to accept a credit card, or tell customers personally where to send the check.

I've seen more sales lost to an mediocre site than Bayer has aspirin. Remember, when someone is looking at your site, looming just over his shoulder are 80,000,000 or so other websites just a few clicks away; and as best as I can figure out, most are more interesting than anything to do with insurance. No offense. In fact, I've written an article, "Don't Send People To Your Web Site," which is yours free, if you drop me a letter requesting it. No, no emails - I need your request on real letterhead as I have a wood burning stove and need the fuel.

While you're sending that request in, don't forget, you can also order my book for $39.95 (+$5)- How To Market A Product For Under $500!, or my second book, Uncommon Marketing Techniques, for just $17.95 (+$4). Or check them out at your local library——if not in stock they can order it in for you. Or, read additional articles at www.dobkin.com. The funnier stuff is in the member's only section. Hold still: "Poof, you are now a member." Congratulations. Oh, yea...

it's five bucks a year - pay up. Order from Danielle Adams Publishing, P.O. Box 100, Merion Station, PA 19066.

To maintain a web presence

Some people like to stay on that cutting edge of technology. Others, like myself, prefer to stay in the dark until the technology is well proven or pver powers everything else. Yesterday, I bought a fax machine.

It's a good thing I didn't listen to the soothsayers about the Internet taking over all marketing functions. I'm actually glad I didn't jump into the web early - I would have spent countless hours on the next new wave of marketing that was poised to take over the world, and put newspapers and magazines out of business — and probably would have crashed like most of the other dotcoms after raising 10 million in venture capital, having fun buying all kinds of neat stuff, then wasting the next 3 years of my life trying to figure out where all the money went. This way, I've just wasted 3 years without any money and without figuring anything out. At my age, I probably would have forgotten most of it by now anyhow. At least I don't have dementia. Or, do I?

To capture email addresses

One of the most valuable assets of your firm is the mailing list of your customers. It's through this revenue source that you continue the privilege of staying in business. You can also increase your revenue by selling customers more stuff, and gathering referrals to get more customers - so you can sell them more stuff, too. To your current customers, you are a proven, trusted resource. Any arguments? Oops, sorry I had to ask you about arguing, my wife has been away for a few days...

The second most valuable asset in your business is your prospect list. It's this list where you have the opportunity to expand your business. The third most valuable asset? It's that cute little red haired girl who sits next to the copy machine. Wow. Everyone says your employees are your most valuable asset and now I see why. 30,000 copies a month, all made by... her. I just throw them out that night when she leaves, and then next day tell her to make more. What? What's wrong with the make-work project. Teddy Roosevelt did it. The fourth most valuable asset, when you get around to it, is the email addresses of people visiting your site.

It's through this low cost marketing medium you can create additional business. The era of prudent use of email is just beginning to take shape. I'm not talking about sending the emails that clutter your inbox now - about enlarging your penis, or is it just me who has a small... well how would they know that? And my breasts are just the right size, also - so whomever is sending those emails, you can stop now, or include better photos. But, do any of those penis enlargement things work? I mean really - I saw one for just $9.95...

The new age of email I'm talking about is real, one-to-one, personal communication——that you can email to thousands of your closest friends and best prospects, just like we do now with personal letters in the direct mail industry.

I often write personal notes and letters to thousands of people, but when each individual gets my letter, he or she gets the feeling they are the only person in the world receiving it. Although most acknowledge somewhere in the back of their mind that others are receiving the same communication, it still largely remains a one-to-one piece of correspondence. That's the beauty of direct mail. And that can be the beauty of email, when you do it right. But it's an art form: to deliver a message in a personal way. Which means: you can do it, but it takes more than 3 minutes to write and design. The whole campaign starts with capturing their email address.

What really counts in virtual reality?

To actually make money on the web, your website must be set up for it, at a cost and expense to automate everything. Then you must be prepared to follow up all this technology with an effort, and credible material - which is still further expense. Wow. Effort, investment, expense, automatic quoting, automatic ordering, no human intervention... is this any way to run a business? All this automation... sounds like work. Heck, if I wanted to work that hard, I can do that without automation.

For the technology enabled, yes - it can be quite profitable. And the best part about it is that a firm can test everything in real time. What would take my direct marketing clients three or four weeks to test in direct mail may take an afternoon on the Internet. We can start seeing early results in an hour.

For the technology challenged, like myself, the revenue Internet models look good on paper, but call me old fashioned, I still like establishing a relationship with clients. And, I think that's true of the insurance industry, too.

I talk on the phone with clients about their needs. Sometimes we play golf - I shoot in the mid-80s, if it gets any hotter than that I don't go out. I can assess what they really need - as opposed to what they've asked for - to see if I can get them a better overall value, perhaps even at a lower price. Then I can over-deliver on service. The Internet model seems to be fixated strictly on price.

Building a relationship with a client takes you out of the "lowest bidder" category and places you into a "good value for the money" category. I know with my own vendors, I wouldn't trade some of them in for the lowest bidder at any cost. Some have helped me immensely. Others have given me sage advice. I've been close friends with my printer for 30 years, and while I'm sure his prices are fair, I'm also sure they're not the lowest unless I ask him for his absolute lowest price (which I do during lean times.) Over the years he's shown me how and where to save on printing, sometimes at his own expense.

And my own personal insurance agent? Been with her over 23 years. She shows me how to submit my needs to the underwriters for the lowest possible quote. And after 10 years, when I finally did submit a claim, she showed me how to do it with the best possible chance of having it paid in full.

And that's the real saving I want. Saving me from headaches. Peace of mind. Isn't that the real value of insurance?

So, where was I? Oh yes, making your phone ring.

I mentioned that your in-house mailing list was your firm's most valuable asset. There are a lot of other lists out there that can be used for prospecting. Lists of names and addresses, sometimes appended with other such data as phone number, age, income, business, position, even policy ex-dates can be purchased through a variety of sources.

In the pursuit of a great response to a mailing, you've got to mail to the list of people who are most likely to make a purchase. The selection of a list, like the choice of a spouse, is important: you are going to have to live with your franchise for a long time. Shop carefully. Unlike shopping for a spouse, shopping for a list isn't fun at all. But, here's some help:

Places to buy mailing lists include list brokers, found in the phone book under, well, list brokers. National list brokers can be found in the direct marketing trade magazines such as Target Marketing (215/238-5300), Direct Marketing Magazine (516/746-6700), and DM News (212/741-2095). Call them for a sample issue. For an article I've written entitled, "Free Catalogs of Mailing Lists;" follow the procurement procedure earlier in this article. For the other 4 or 5 articles I've written on lists, send me 3 bucks. If you make money from this article, be a sport - send me 5 bucks.

Two good mailing list resources found at your local library are the Oxbridge Communication Directory of Mailing Lists, and the SRDS Directory of Mailing Lists. Each book is the size of the Manhattan yellow pages. Both warehouse the names, addresses and phone numbers of about 30,000 lists that are available for rent.

Almost all catalog merchandisers rent their mailings lists of buyers and inquirers. They offer selects such as hot line buyers (buyers who have purchased with the last 30 days, 60 day, 90 days). In addition to a selection of recency of purchase, they also offer selections by amount of purchase, category purchase, and multi-buyers to name but a few.

90% of magazine publishers sell their lists. These names can be quite focused in a particular niche market or industry segment. Addresses are unusually current, when a publisher gets a magazine back it's expensive for them - so the recurring problem of non-deliverable names is addressed early in a publisher's career, and bad names (nixies) are removed promptly.

While I'm writing about marketing to a particular industry, most trade associations sell their lists of members. The State and Regional Associations Directory ($199) and The National Trade and Professional Associations of the United States ($299) from Columbia Books, Inc. (888-265-0600; www.co-lumbiabooks.com) are good resources. And the motherload of association directories, the Encyclopedia of Associations (The Gale Group, 800-877-GALE) shows detailed information on more than 23,000 local, state, national, and international associations. The three books in the Gale set are about $500, but they are awesome.

If you're the "I'll find the data myself" kind of person, InfoUSA (800/321-0869) offers a Searchable CD of just about everyone and everything in the US. It's actually pretty good.

Trade show exhibitors and trade show attendees can be found at the resource of The Tradeshow Week Data Book (213-965-5300), published by the editors of Tradeshow Week Magazine. Another great trade show directory is the website of trade show central - tscentral, now called TSNN.com

Lists of selected local businesses can be found at the local chamber of commerce, or at Cole's Directories (www.experian.com) which also gives addresses by location. You can get businesses segmented by zip code, street address, number of employees, size of facility, type of firm, SIC, income, whatever. With this resource, you can rent a list of all businesses on a particular street, in sequence of their address.

Business lists are most commonly rented for $65 TO $95 per thousand, with $85/M being the mean. (Resident lists of just addresses, no names, is about $20/M) Adding overlays such as phone numbers, as well as demographics, income, purchase history, ethnic background and so forth each add to the cost, usually about $10/M per overlay. Names are usually rented for one-time usage and are seeded to detect abuse. You'll most likely have to rent 5,000 names, but this doesn't mean you have to mail to all 5,000. With smaller firms, I recommend testing smaller quantities.

If you are planning to get a response of over 2%, you need to have one heck of an offer - but more about increasing your direct marketing response rates next month: Sponge Bob is on TV and I think it's episode 49 at the Krusty Crab and... oh never mind—I gotta go. Don't forget, your mailing will be only as good as the list you mail it to. Your list the probably the most crucial factor in the success or failure of your mailing. Hope this has been helpful. See you.

SHOPPING FOR A LIST ON-LINE?

It's 1:48 AM and I can't sleep. 80 Channels of nothing good is on TV. My kids hid their Gameboy Advance from me, and I can't find the controller for the Nintendo so I guess I'll get a little work done. Sound familiar? So... your kids hide the Gameboy from you, too?

Sitting by the cold glow of the CRT, I looked up "Mailing Lists" on the Google search engine and came up with more matches than Bayer has aspirin. The top sponsored spot (they paid for that top slot with the little box around it) was for "Cheap Mailing Lists" from directmailconnection.com. OK, I like "cheap", as long as it isn't "inferior".

With one small click I challenged them to change my life and the way I think about researching mailing lists forever. Zoom, I was in. I looked up opportunity seekers from their database of 4900 yellow pages and 500 white pages phone books they said they use. No other sourcing was apparent. Funny, I didn't know you could get opportunity seekers from the white pages, or there even was an "Opportunity Seekers" heading in the Yellow Pages. Maybe in California - they seem to get everything first.

Undaunted, I clicked further. The cost was $65/M - or you could buy 100 names for $15. I dunno... If you only have 15 bucks to throw at a direct mail test, better not quit your day job just yet. On the upside, 10,000 names cost $450. But it was their guarantee that scared me off: they'd send you 2 names for every one that came back. I don't like cleaning someone else's mailing list at my cost of 41¢ for each wrecked and returned mailing piece I receive back. So I left "cheap" in search of "better." It was 2:00 AM, 12 minutes later.

Back at Google, Listbazaar.com (InfoUSA) also came up at the top of paid spots. They offered selections from a db of

12 million businesses, 250 million consumers, and also will sell me a CD Directory of phone books. Bleary eyed, I wasn't quite ready for that yet.

Undaunted by my resistance, they then tried to close me on a "Customer Analyzer," which carried a $250 price tag, then cost an additional $250 for 500 names - which I passed on quite readily, thank you. Being anonymous really does have its advantages, you know. It was late and I was tired, not stupid.

Continuing on the InfoUSA site, I tried to look up motorcycle dealers and found no matches. After discarding the brief assumption there are no motorcycle dealers in the U.S., somehow I got to S.I.C. 5571-06 Motorcycle and Scooter Dealers-Honda. Now I know why I stumbled: InfoUSA has a preference for Honda.

I clicked my way towards a count of dealers in a 20 mile radius of my house in downtown Bala-Cynwyd PA (4 blocks outside of Philadelphia in case you've never heard of beautiful downtown Bala-Cynwyd - home of the famous... uh... well, home to many people who are nice.) I asked for a radius of 20 miles and found I could buy the full records of dealers for $10.80, or the base records of dealers for $6. Exit, stage left, at 2:16, 16 minutes later. I vowed I come back here one day, and I do for a more serious review of this site by the end of this research. A single thought I'd forget about entirely by the time I go to bed, just a few minutes later.

After a brief stint at Google and a scan down the list of mailing list URLs, I went to Accurateleads.com (Dimark) 800-865-4787. Their site runs off of 40,000 databases, which sounded pretty extensive to me. So I click on S.I.C. code information and a mini-screen pops up asking me to save the file in RTF format. Thinking this means "Release Toxic Formula," I decline. Besides, no sense clogging my 60 gig hard drive with this kind of heavy 75K file. Heck, I'm almost at half a gig now and I've only had this computer for less than two and a half years.

I click on their "Tips" rollover and find it's under development. I make a mental note to call them sometime between later and much later to offer them my direct marketing tips booklet (you can have one too - call 610-642-1000 and request it) for their site content. Apparently at this late hour my mind is under development, too, as I completely forget about this too until proofing this article.

They offer about 50 specialty lists, and offer counts - but not in real time (they'll call me tomorrow with the count). So, with a click and a whoosh, I head out at 2:23, just 7 minutes later.

Back at Google I fumble through several more sites unproductively - PAML.net which is email lists only; Apple, another email only list, then finally land on #11, USADATA which is Acxiom - a pretty familiar name to us DM techies.

Feeling comfortably numb in my robe and fuzzy slippers (shhh, don't tell anyone) before the CRT screen, I go in. Click: Select by state, click: advanced list data, click: 10 to 19 employees and bingo - PA businesses with 10-19 people = a list with 37,233 records which I can buy at 20¢ a name or $7,446.60. Not having my credit card - or $7446.60 - handy, I bludgeon on, completely reading their 20 page agreement. Oh, sorry, I must have dozed off. Since my eyes can't focus all that well late at night I make a mental note to completely read it sometime between later and never, and scroll through their 20 page agreement in about 10 seconds - not being able to focus on a single word. I leave it for others with more time on their hands to read, then proceed directly to step 4 which is pay and get list.

Somehow I feel cheated. Like taking your sister to the prom, I felt I should have at least run across a "thank you" by this time - especially if I was going to plunk down $7,446.60 after being at their site for under 20 minutes. So I looked for the "back" button and... there was no going back. No back button. I guess they figured if I got this far they'd put the pressure on to sign.

Not yet ready to commit to a $7,000 in under 20 minutes purchasing decision, I navigate my way to earlier screens and find pop-up mini-screens keep appearing out of nowhere almost as fast as I can click on their close boxes. It's OK, really - I was feeling a bit dominate by not really waiting for their content to show up. MMmmmm... More power. But alas and alack, clicking around some more, I find I keep returning to the same old screens -- until they finally try to sell me consulting reports from $1,600 to $7,500 a pop, so I leave. It was 2:39, 16 minutes after entering their site. I start dreaming my life is occurring in 16 minute intervals...

I always knew the web was the home of the short attention span theater - and here I am, living proof. This late at night my fuzzy slippers usually start talking to me - telling me to shoot the neighbor's dog that keep barking, but tonight is different, they actually show up with a gun.

Back at Google things were heating up at a the URL of a site of a lesbian mailing list, but without photos I left in short order. Then I wondered if I was going to get emails from all the porn sites like when, umm, my friend, umm, did when he visited a few porn sites. OK, so he visited a few hundred porn sites. Heck, that's who's making all the money on the web: all the porn sites. Don't tell me you've never....... Even once? Just out of curiosity? Yea, right.

So returning to Google I clicked on the site of Gimp.org just to find out what the heck gimp.org was. To my amazement, it was a full blown-out site complete with documentation about, well - I never did figure it out as it was all computer stuff. I guess they got gimp.org because geek.org was taken. Go on - check it out, see if you can figure out what the heck it is.

At the 40th slot at the search engine was ZAPDATA (from IMARKET and D&B). If you haven't heard of ZAPDATA by now, and their offer for 50 free leads - touted in their many mailings and full page advertisements in all the trade rags - where have you been living? So now I figure I must be getting close to the good stuff. I'd go right in to get my 50 free leads.

But noooooo. Before they send me 50 free leads - and I'm not sure exactly what good 50 names from a general mailing list are - they wanted me to register first. And from the looks of the form I was to sign over my first born, give them a full blown marketing plan, and the numbers and passcodes for all my Swiss bank accounts... before I'd be getting 50 stinkin' leads. But first, I'd have to sign off on their privacy policy. If I read it I'd be the first. Even people in Alaska with 180 days of 24 hour nights per year, who are retired, with no cable TV, and have nothing to do but watch the ice recede - don't read this document. Me neither. I left.

My continuing search on Google turned up a spiritual mailing list, but with no actual photos of God or other proof, I left from the site immediately. When a site for a mental health page mailing list came up I feared the worst - they'd capture my name and invite me in. So... I didn't visit.

Then I got smart, and typed Direct+Marketing+ Mailing+Lists" into the search parameters on Google. How clever and I? Well, bam - tons of catalogs came up. Ooops. Not too clever, I guess.

Finally, the "thinkdirectmarketing.com" not-quite-ready-for-prime-time site came up. I clicked on "articles" thinking I could finally learn something - and one article came up. Someone please tell them the "s" on the word articles makes it plural. The "Books" link on their site took me to Amazon... and I never did find a list and left 12 screens and 6 minutes later.

It was getting late - or early - depending on your view of time, and if you have to get up in 4 hours. So I scroll down to dmoz.org/business/marketing/direct_marketing which shows about 100 mailing list links, with one line descriptions of each. Some were familiar names, but some of the biggies were absent - like Info USA (wow how could they miss that one!) and Edith Roman, the firm that sent me the nicest list catalog I've ever received. Hmmmm... Edith Roman...

Knowing the information is out there I typed in EdithRoman.com. and finally found some familiar turf. I had enough clearance from previous client work to fully access counts and databases, so I kinda knew how to get most of the information I needed, but still - like walking your dog and he doesn't, you know, go, the experience left me with a "not quite fully fulfilled" feeling.

While I could get S.I.C. counts and a few demographics with the provided click boxes, I couldn't get multiple overlays that weren't included in their checkbox page. Additional information, and the tough, lean questions about files that I like to ask list vendors was lacking. File usage, not there. Number of file continuations or rollouts, nope. Recency, frequency, monetary, no. Data Card information - yes, for some files. Missing: relationships that you build with list vendors and recommendations you can trust - priceless... and definitely lacking. All in all, the web doesn't do everything - but for basic preliminary list investigations or an hour's entertainment if you're a direct marketing junkie, at 2AM, it's great. Must... sleep... now....

MAKING THE TELEPHONE WORK FOR YOU

Whoever thought I'd get tired of the Sponge-Bob Square Pants Channel -

24 hours a day of Sponge Bob Square Pants?

So I started flicking around the channels and found out there is now a Suzie Oreman Channel - investment advice from a ever-smiling woman whose redeeming quality is that she has more teeth than Barney.

Come to think about it, almost everyone has more teeth than Barney - he only has one tooth that goes across the entire front of his mouth. So I meant she has bigger teeth. Or... well, whatever. She seems to be on PBS about 12 hours a day. Maybe she gets lessons from Barney, who dominates the other 12 hours of PBS programming, now that they discovered the purple Teletubby really was gay. I wonder if the same people who created Barney created her?

Anyhow, I was a bit loaded and a little tired, so I grabbed a stack of magazines and headed off into the reading room. As I flipped through the pages of old Playboys, Hustlers and an occasional copy of Modern Nudest magazines... (hey, don't give me that look - I just get it for the articles) I chanced upon a copy of a direct marketing trade magazine and became intensely interested in a column blasting telemarketers. What? Don't tell me you don't get Modern Nudest, I reviewed all the magazines you get in your credit file on-line. I wouldn't worry about that as much as the sub-prime rating you have...

Telemarketing, like spam, sucks - but it can be effective. But... My God, man... the article was correct. Telemarketing guys don't get blasted enough - especially from people in my own direct marketing industry. And damn it, they should - they deserve it.

Sure, they call themselves direct marketers. And I usually have a lot of compassion for most other direct marketers: we send stuff to you in the mail, you don't like it, you throw it away. Or you use it to fuel that wood burning stove. But you don't have to get up early to answer it, and you're probably not reading it right in the middle of your dinner - that special time is reserved for fighting with your wife and yelling at the kids. Somehow this outbound telephone soliciting niche of our direct marketing profession doesn't get any sympathy from me.

You know what I hate? No, even worse than slow drivers who leave their turn signals on. No, worse than that, too - and besides I don't think it's all that kinky, especially if you take the handcuffs off after only half an hour.

I hate telephone sales reps who ask me how I am. I'd tell them, but who has an extra few hours to listen to an old guy gripe. But what I really can't stand, what pushes me over the top, is the recorded messages from telemarketer's automated calling machines.

It wasn't invasive enough for telemarketing firms to get me up several times from dinner with my family to try to let me know my TV Guide subscription is going to run out in just 7 months, or to make sure I knew the latest offer to have my rugs cleaned; now they have predictive dialers and voice recognition. Unhampered by human intervention, they can now call thousands of people and annoy them without enduring the costs or burnout of real people to make the calls.

Usually after grumbling a few words and cussing when the first recording que comes up, I reluctantly give up at being mad at a machine. I think of the people who listen to the response and laugh at the cursing and how mad people must really be to get these calls. I'm sure they then talk about programing their phone dialers to give the complainer

40,000 calls between 2AM and 6AM. Don't laugh - I've had a fax machine dial my house several times at 3 in the morning. I was livid.

As long as I'm bitchin',* one more thing. I just love answering the phone with my name, Jeffrey Dobkin, only to hear some idiot ask for Jeffrey Dobkin. Similar to getting mad at a machine for calling you at random, getting pissed at people that are as stupid as an automated dialer, or too ill-trained to vary from their script even for a few nanoseconds isn't in my composition - so with my anger stuffed inside of me to be taken out on some unsuspecting employee or my children, whoever is closest at the time, the phone calls are merely brief:

"Jeff Dobkin."

"Hello may I speak with Jeff Dobkin?"

"Sigh... Is this a soliciting call?'

"No."

"What do you want?"

"Is Jeff Dobkin there?"

"This is Robert Dodge of the Lower Merion police department. How do you know Jeff Dobkin?"

Long pause.

"This is a soliciting call."

Besides, before you can really let go with a full stream of consciousness, the TSRs almost always hang up. Some are even rude enough to disconnect without so much as a thank you for your time, or even saying goodbye as soon as you say you're not really interested in yet another jar of penis enlargement cream. (Hey, the jar I bought off the Internet worked when I rubbed it in... well for the first few minutes, anyhow...) "Time is money" says TSR Today Magazine. God, it seems like every psychopath has his own magazine these days.

Still, I feel violated, and cheap whenever I do that to myself. Oh, sorry, I was speaking about something else.

At work, different problems emerge: I get mad from the intrusion of a telemarketer calling and asking for me by my first name. Don't get me wrong - I'm usually the last in line for any kind of formal protocol, and I actually prefer to be called Jeffrey... as calling me Mr. Dobkin makes me think of my dad - an old guy - strangely enough, similarly named. But here's the exception: calling me Jeffrey under the false pretense to get by my secretary under the guise of the false pretense that they know me on a first name basis. That possibly is the absolute worst way to get me to buy something, anything from their firm - by disbanding any possible element of trust very early in the conversation. Most thieves usually wait until after they have my Visa or M/C number. My wife just waits until I'm asleep to go through my wallet.

I'm usually not a supporter of governmental legislation to police industries, but I support the no-calling laws that are now passing around a multitude of states' legislatures. The industry wasn't responsible enough to police itself, and now must suffer the heavy hand of governmental restriction. At least I can eat dinner in peace now, and watch Sponge Bob without telephone interruption.

Wow, that's a lot of complaining. But that's not what I've come here to talk about. I just got off the phone to talk about what a telemarketing campaign can do for your firm. Remember? Like spam, it works - with the emphasis on "it works." And there's even a way to do it nicely. Certain restrictions apply, but let's take a look at a few good uses of the phone.

The Phone can be a great personal service to customers

When you make the call yourself, the telephone is great for keeping up with that personal relationship with your customers and clients. It's a one-on-one open dialog that can increase consumer retention and trust, and increase the lifetime value of a customer.

But, with customers that you don't speak with - except once every couple of years, or when there's a problem with their account, an outbound personal phone call carries a lot of weight and can be construed as "Why is he calling me, something must be wrong." So, I feel a personal call from you is not only unnecessary, it's unwarranted; and I don't recommend it. Instead - to maintain contact, strangely enough, I'd have a staff person call the client. It's simply more appropriate.

I'd make the courtesy call around the time of the expiration of the policy. Key points to this call: Have the caller identify him or her self as a customer service manager for your firm; say this is a courtesy call from (and insert your name,) to let you know your policy has remained in effect for the past year and you have had full uninterrupted coverage as specified. Your new policy will take effect at 12PM on ___, with no lapse in coverage or protection.

I'd also have the TSR ask if there are any questions about premiums or policies and express the desire to answer same or offer to call back with an exact answer to a specific question. I'd close by saying "We know it is a privilege to have your business and we appreciate it; it's our goal to provide excellent service to you, to be here anytime you need us, and we thank you for the opportunity to be your agent, and for your trust."

After the conversation, the TSR sends the client a letter thanking them for receiving his phone call, saying it was a pleasure speaking with him, even if it wasn't. It continues throughout the letter, thanking the customer for their business, letting them know that your agency "is always on its toes ready to immediately assist you or any of your friends or associates with any questions about insurance or insurance related products." Inserting "you or any of your friends or associates" is a powerful but subtle way to get referrals, which is the secondary objective of this letter. The primary objective of this letter - although hidden - is to ask for a quote for other insurance products.

It's very, very tricky to ask to quote other insurance needs in a thank-you letter. The reason being: if you ask directly it negates ANY and ALL of the positive aspects of the letter. So, how do you do this? For the answer - simple as it is, send $2 to Jeff Dobkin, PO Box 100, Merion Station, PA 19066. Thanks.

If the client asks your TSR a question that's too tough, or if the customer is too tough, offer to have you (the principal) call them back: what time would be convenient for them? The nature of the staff person calling is to save you time, not to disassociate you from the customer. Only 5% or so of clients will want to speak with you directly and you should be readily available and eager to speak with them. When you do talk with them, this increases the bond between you and your customer, and increases the value of the relationship and the value of doing business with your firm.

So instead of making 300 calls a week, you are only speaking with 15 customers a week who have actual questions - but still getting the personal mileage of a very positive customer contact by phone. This is a telemarketing campaign done right. It's like sex: everybody feels good after it, both you and your sister; er, customers, umm, partners, er, partner. Unfortunately your TSR will need psychiatric help after 15 months of burning himself out by making 60 calls a day. Oh well. If life really was fair... all the impersonators would be dead and Elvis would be alive.

If you want to get personal with each of your clients, write them a letter of thanks. That's right, a letter of thanks can be more personal - and more effective - than a phone call. If you do it right.

The letter of thanks should simply state "Thanks for the opportunity to provide service to you. We know there is a choice of insurance providers, and it is our privilege to have you select us as both a provider and a friend. If we can ever be of any assistance in any insurance-related matter, call me personally at anytime. Thanks again for your business and your trust."

Here's your two bucks worth.

OK, ok, for all you crybabies that actually read the earlier part of this article, then got mad at me for saying there is a charge for this (I know: it's just information, and everything is free), then you started to write to the publisher to complain "oh, that Jeff Dobkin is... blah blah blah - he wanted us to send him two bucks to tell us blah blah blah..." I will now tell you whiners a few correct ways to sneak-in a request for getting more business by asking for a quote in a thank you letter. You can, um, send me the two bucks later.

3. Include a survey. Dress the survey up so that it looks like a "How can we be of better service to you" survey, but load-in one or two really important questions that you want answered, the first one offering a check box and an under-lined area for: "May we have the privilege of quoting any other insurance needs?" To encourage clients to complete it, I would also offer a small gift for the return of the completed survey.

2. In the PS of your letter, understate your request for a quote. "Have a question? Need a quick quote? We are always pleased to be of immediate help. Just call us at:_____" and print your phone number here. I know, I know, your phone number is in the letterhead. Place it here anyhow: you want to encourage phone calls don't you - (this is the primary objective of this letter) and an additional phone number is a great way to increase them. BTW, the secondary objective of the letter is to enhance the customer's relationship with your firm to create a stronger loyalty bond.

1. Have a short statement soliciting quotes that looks like part of the stationery. If the body of your letter is set in courier typeface, set flush left rag right (FLRR) as it should be, have the RFQ (Request For Quote) set in Bookman, New Century Schoolbook, or Helvetica type - or follow your own designer's letterhead or logo typeface. Drop this line in the upper right hand corner of the stationery, so it looks like a printed part of your letterhead. "For Immediate Quotes Call 987-654-3211".

You can also have this RFQ on the bottom of the page. Again, set in a contrasting style of type - different from the body copy in your letter. When presented at the bottom of the letterhead, this line should be centered. You know how some businesses have their address printed on the bottom of the page? This line should be printed directly above or below that address line in the same typestyle - so it looks like it's part of the printed stationery.

When the RFQ is designed-in to be subtle, it doesn't destroy the integrity of the letter, or dilute the perception - or the delusion - that this is simply a "thank you for your business" letter.

The EX Date and Limited Time offers

Most telephone calls in the insurance industry are centered around the policy ex-date. When the ex-date of a policy is coming up it gives you a non-threatening reason to call your client and offer them the convenience of continual coverage without interruption. When phrased like this, who could get mad at a caller? You're saving them from the exposure of -gasp- a lapse in coverage.

Another justification for calling customers is an offer limited by time. "Since this limited time offer couldn't wait another few days until you received it by mail, we are calling to let our better customers know of the availably of this special offer." An example of this occurrence may be if additional coverage is offered by one of our providers, and "in order for our customers to be able to take advantage of the special savings, we needed to let customers know about it immediately - so you could make the decision about this yourself before the offer is rescinded or our supplier runs out of gifts.

The "limited by time" offer - if created with the good credibility of "time is running out - we had to get this too-good-to-pass-up offer to you right away" also gives justification to fax someone. While I usually discourage broadcasting faxes because of their invasive, intrusive nature, if you're gonna broadcast a fax, at least it should be effective for you. So use something that gives the appearance of "time is running out quickly!"

Lastly, remember, almost every phone call should be followed up by a letter. Because long after the phone call is forgotten, if you've confirmed it in a letter, you've created a document in someone's file to remind him of you, your firm, and how great it is doing business with you. The letter can sit on someone's desk for a day or two, or a couple of months if it's anything like my desk - a constant reminder of what a pleasure it is doing business with your firm. A permanent record of your wonderfulness. A final note to your greatness emblazoned on a... oh never mind, you get the idea.

There are other telemarketing programs that are successful, but... The Simpsons is on....

Jeff Dobkin

Sorry about the word "bitchin'". I just wanted to see how a professional website handled an apostrophe and a comma - all typeset next to each other... And now an apostrophe, a quote mark and a period.

CREATING AN EFFECTIVE CUSTOMER SERVICE PLAN

It is a privilege to service your customers. With this thought in both your mind and in your heart, you will be successful in customer service. But having a plan helps to really succeed.

Depending on the size of your company, you will need an informal (small company) to formal plan consisting of not only policies and procedures (boring), but also key phrases of how you would like your customers addressed and spoken to. Start taking notes when you are on the phone.

You should specify your company's key phrases in a written document for all employees to learn. Start this three-ring binder now. Ya' see, you know exactly what you like to say to customers, now your employees and associates can address customers this very same way. It is necessary to write these phrases down, once they are logged in a book it will perpetuate the way you prefer employees to speak about the issues at hand.

For example, in my old direct mail firm we mailed over 1,000 orders a week. As you can imagine, everything that could possibly happen to an order that goes through the mail happened to us. Our largest complaint was the merchandise was not received.

Our policy for non-receipt was established very early: first we verified the order and the shipping date. Our policy was to wait two weeks, in case the order was merely delayed and not lost, then ship a replacement. If the call was received after the two-week time period, we would manufacture and ship a replacement at no charge to the customer that same day.

Further, if we couldn't verify their order, we asked they read us over the phone our endorsement from the back of their check. I figured if they knew what our endorsement said, in all likelihood we cashed their check. Every telephone sales rep at our shop knew our procedures and regurgitated them to each customer in the identical way as problems arose.

Our policy for a product that was not to the customer's 100% satisfaction was different: the product was immediately replaced at no charge with our next model up, sent same day.

By devising these policies up-front, we handled every case of non-delivery in a consistent fashion. When a customer called, everyone in our firm always responded with the same key phrases. We asked for the customer's zip code, "May I have the zip code the product was shipped to, please." The TSR looked up the order and said, "I'm sorry you didn't receive your order, we mailed it to..." – and we gave their address so they knew we sent it, and gave the date it was mailed.

These simple solutions appeased customers in several ways. We created credibility by giving them their own street address when all they gave us was their name and zip code. We let them know if their merchandise didn't arrive within two weeks, no problemo sending a new one, free. And if anyone called back and said someone promised something different, we were all sure the customer was remembering a conversation he had with another firm. The chain of command? Angry callers went to the floor manager. Further dissatisfied customers got right to me. How did our service policy work? Less than one customer in 10,000 requested a refund. In fact, five refunds in a year would have been a lot.

Customer service addresses two distinct situations: 1. how the customer is handled when the order goes correctly;

and 2. what happens when something screws up. Your goal with either scenario is to receive feedback so that you know what the customer thinks of the service your firm provides. Regardless of how you feel, it is each customer that determines his or her satisfaction with your customer service. Your goal: constant improvement at whatever level your firm maintains.

Normal Orders

We'll start with the easy one. Each customer and each order has a flow path which may be charted. The phone rings, or an order comes in by mail or fax... now what? Big companies have a strictly set policy for every event so that decisions do not have to be made each time an order is received. As problems arise, the procedure manual is revised to keep the flow smooth and to alert new employees how to handle the unexpected. Small firms can learn from this technique of efficient order processing.

Charting the flow path of normal orders not only increases efficiency but also assigns employee responsibility for each part of order processing and product flow. If there's a bottleneck or a mistake that is made consistently, the flow path will show it quickly. Following is flow path of orders for my old firm, but it could be for any firm. Each function was assigned to a distinct group which was responsible for a particular part of the operation, from ensuring a smooth flow of information and goods to correctly handling its part in the manufacturing and shipping chain.

Mail Opened ' Cashiering ' Orders Separated and Batched ' Processing and Data Entry ' Manufacturing ' Final Audit and Inspection ' Assembly ' Final Check ' Mailing.

Measuring Results

Depending on the value of each order or each customer, a customer satisfaction device as simple as a postcard that is included with each order or with your product instructions may give you a non-intrusive way to find out what your customers really think about your firm. I recommend this simple and inexpensive device. A customer satisfaction survey may also be included as part of your warranty registration card.

For orders of greater dollar amounts, a double-sided postcard sent to customers when you receive their warranty registration card will give you an idea of your customers' satisfaction with your service. In addition, since they've now had time to try out your product, you can find out their satisfaction with that, too. If you include a nicely written letter when you send this card to customers, it will show you really do care and will build loyalty and trust.

If the order value is high enough, a phone call is always appreciated after the sale, to thank the customer and to make sure everything is OK. Car dealers that do this get repeat customers. Physicians who do this build their practices faster. It's the best PR program a firm can have. For really big sales, the salesperson should call on the client personally, on occasion. For really, really big sales, the salesperson should take the client on your boat, on occasion. If this article is of great help in securing and retaining really, really big clients, you should take me on your boat.

Here's where the problems start.

When things go awry, a good customer service program can save your butt, your customers, and grief. One person or team should be assigned to handle customer problems. For customer problems not resolved at this first level (dollar amount too high, outstanding machinery problems, problem customers), a higher level of authority such as a manager or senior manager should be assigned. In my firm, although they were few, I fielded all the irate customers.

Format: Customer service representative

1. Listen to grievance in entirety. This is an important step.

2. Tell customer you understand why they feel the way they do. "I understand how mad you must be. I'll try to find a solution so you're totally satisfied. I'll do everything in my

power to help." (Never, ever say "That's our policy" or "That's the way it's always been done here.")

3. Ask customer what they would like - their own solution. "What would you like us to do to resolve this for you right now?" Or, "If you offer a suggestion or a solution, I'll be happy to listen."

4. When resolution is proposed, restate it, ask if that is correct. If the customer's proposed resolution is acceptable, agree. Ask customer if he is satisfied with the resolution.

Send "Thank you for the opportunity to be of further help" card, with "Was this resolved to your satisfaction?" bounce-back to create a paper trail.

5. If the resolution authority is exceeded, explain that additional permission is needed, and offer to call complainant back at their convenience. ("I'm sorry, that resolution is above my level of authority, but I'll be happy to propose this to my manager and call you back by five this afternoon. Would that be all right?"

6. If resolution is permitted, repeat steps four and five.

7. If resolution is not permissible, explain why (over dollar limit, not practical) and try to have two optional offers to complete the resolution at that time. If first is accepted, see above. If rejected, have final back-up offer ready. Secondary offer should be well thought-out. If accepted, see above.

8. If the customer still does not accept the resolution, tell the caller you "understand their position" and are sorry you could not resolve this to their satisfaction. Tell them you will have a senior manager call them. Ask again for their proposal to resolve this matter to their satisfaction – tell them you need this so that you can write what they say down to give to your manager. This gives customers a final chance to recognize if this resolution is silly or absurd, and a last out, knowing it will be presented to management. This also lessens customer anger. Give proposal to manager with case details. Create paper trail of what was done.

Flow path

Customer service rep ' resolution; if yes, ask if resolved to customer satisfaction, thank customer for opportunity to be of service, send thank you card or gift certificate.

Not resolved ' mid-manager ' resolution (as above); not resolved ' senior management ' resolution (as above); not resolved ' VP need resolution (as above); not resolved ' make final settlement offer. (The VP initially sets responsibility levels and dollar limits of all employees handling complaints.)

Each step of the customer service resolution process must be documented on paper or computer archive in case of real or imagined litigation. I recommend a paper trail be initiated with a complaint number (which may just be the date, or the date followed by the customer number) so files may be reviewed by management, or be kept for litigation purposes.

Steps to an Effective Customer Service Plan

1. Recognition of service effort needed.

Some firms have continual service headaches, others never a call. Establish procedures up-front to ensure each customer gets the same fair treatment, and to protect employees from irate customers.

2. Determine level of service needed.

Assign resolution responsibility to each level of employee for different levels of dollar sales and different levels of customers.

3. Create benchmarks to measure plan effectiveness.

4. Measure level of consumer and business-to-business satisfaction.

5. Adjust plan.

6. Recognize additional efforts.

Reward employees who outperform stated customer satisfaction objectives and goals. Make sure they share success stories via written documentation which is submitted to management.

Reward employees who make recommendations of how to handle complaints better, how to be more effective, or who consistently offer better ways and procedures.

7. Show appreciation of spectacular customer satisfaction efforts by employees with "employee of the month", movie tickets, special parking privileges, hours off, days off, dinner out, medals, trophies, bonus, and of course verbal praise.

8. Hold regular "customer satisfaction" meetings.

Ask employees what else they recommend doing for their customers to increase customer satisfaction in the first place and to establish better company loyalty from customers. This will stimulate employees to think in terms of: "What else can we do for our customers?"

As it turns out, customer service not only applies to your customers, it applies to your employees as well. In our old direct marketing firm, the lifetime value of a customer was about $100. But the value of a responsive, well-liked, and hard-working employee was much greater. Much, much greater.

So what's the bottom line? Customer service is a phrase that applies to a state of mind in which you are constantly thinking of every facet of your business where people – customers and employees – are involved. It's finding a way to make sure all are satisfied with your corporate entity and would enjoy continuing to do business with you. It should employ a method of measuring and tracking this feeling of loyalty and a program to ensure its continual evolution to higher levels.

What does all this mean? Take an example of the L.L. Bean Company, a firm that sends out well over 60 million catalogs a year. Several years ago my brother asked if I would return a pair of shoes for him when they didn't fit. So I did. After three months, I called them and told them I was disappointed his charge slip was not credited for the return. A credit was issued immediately, without question. The following month when I found the box with the new shoes in it under a remote table in my living room, so I sent the shoes back (really) with a short note of apology and thanks.

As a customer who has seen their customer service level firsthand, I purchase about half my clothing from Bean. My lifetime value as a customer? A lot. Do I have a good bit of customer loyalty? You bet. Do I ever recommend them? All the time (as I write this article!). The bottom line of great customer service is this: do customers ever recommend your firm to others?

BUILDING LOYALTY AND CUSTOMER RETENTION FOR UNDER A DOLLAR

The buzzword for this week is "branding." Last week it was "Brand Loyalty." Oh yeah, and the buzz-acronym for this week is "CRM." Customer Retention Management. What crap.

What? Do you new guys on the marketing block think we old guys didn't know what we were doing ten, twenty years ago. Do you think we didn't know how to keep a customer? So you came up with a new name for it, am I supposed to be impressed? Hell, there's even a "Branding" magazine now, and a preachy new "CRM Magazine." Ooooh. Look what's neeeew. Excuuusseee meeeeee.

You want to see a good example of CRM, take a look at L.L. Bean. They've been around forever - and they keep their customers... for life. They've been marketing extremely well without all the new buzzwords, thank you. And I assure you they've been around a lot longer than any new fangled "Customer Retention Management" scheme.

Shamefully, most big companies today actually do need to study "CRM" - cause they don't know shit about keeping customers happy. Just take a look at Sprint, or AT&T, or any of the big phone companies. You get their worst prices if you're a loyal, long-term customer. Exactly what were those connivers thinking to concoct that plan? Then, call them with a quick question... and get... 20 minutes of voice mail. Finally, they blow you off to their website so you can spend four hours looking for something it would have taken them 30

seconds to answer on the phone. I wonder if there's a secret publication called Anti-CRM Magazine that only the phone companies - and credit card companies - receive? And banks. And...

Yeah, so the phone companies have got to read up on it. They lose so many people on the back-end that they have to continually market on the front-end to stay ahead. I guess they haven't figured out that it costs about one fifth as much to keep a current customer as it costs to acquire a new one. Heck, they could blow their marketing costs out of the water if they could get their fingers out of their noses long enough to write a few thank you letters. But I'm getting a little ahead of myself.

If you ask me, and some firms do, the way to keep customers is with good old-fashioned honesty, and some good old-fashioned service. (I know, it's quite a stretch for some of the phone companies!) You answer the phone when it rings - with a real, live person. You don't tell customers the crap about "...to give you better service the phone call is being recorded." Yeah, right. And here's three more quick lessons: You build a brand by providing good value: first quality products and services. You build customer retention by asking customers if there's anything else you can do for them - then doing it. And you create loyalty when you thank them sincerely when they buy something from you.

When you do all this on a regular basis, do you know what you get? Presto! Customer Retention. You develop a customer who keeps buying your goods and services. Poof! Brand Loyalty. And a customer who tells his friends about you: Bingo! Company Loyalty.

And now, I'm going to tell you how to get all these things for under $1. First, you send me a dollar and... just kidding. You do it in a letter.

A letter is the most effective single sheet of paper in direct marketing. It has been since I started my direct marketing career way back in, well, never you mind; and it will be long after I finish this column, which right about now will have to wait until after Sponge Bob SquarePants. Yes, and a letter will still be the most effective tool in direct marketing way after Jay Leno is off the air, and when The Simpsons shows its final episode. Well, maybe not The Simpsons.

What makes a letter such a powerful tool? And how do you create one that has this kind of effect? It's easy - I'll show you.

In direct marketing a letter isn't really a letter. A letter is something you write to Aunt Bertha at Thanksgiving so you get a nice gift at Christmas. In direct marketing a letter is really a one page highly stylized ad designed to look like a letter. Any arguments?

When you write a letter the very first thing you write is... the objective. What do you want to accomplish from this letter. If the letter goes perfectly according to plan, what will the immediate result be? That's the objective. Draft your whole letter around that.

Take this quick test: take a look at most of your correspondence. What's the objective? Most people are probably saying it's to generate a sale; unless you're a lawyer - in which case it's to sue some poor bastard - in which case God says, "so ye shall reap what ye shall sow." And I say it takes one to know one. Well, I guess that pissed off all the lawyers who are now either not reading the rest of this column or who are busy figuring out if I am liable for the above heretofore, or... are already preparing to send me a notice of suit. Good riddance to you. Do you know what you have when you have 8 lawyers buried in the sand up to their necks? Not enough sand. (Hey, just kidding, can't you guys take a joke?) Some of my best friends are, umm, ok, never mind.

So you create letters to sell. Sell sell sell. Sell products, services, appointments, sales calls. Right? OK, now those of you who shook their heads yes, reach out and smack yourself on the butt. Unless you are a direct marketer and your customers read your letters and directly send you money with an order, your real objective isn't to sell your product. People don't read your letter and send you money. The real objective is to generate a phone call. Your letter simply makes the phone ring. When the phone rings, the letter worked - perfectly. It fulfilled the objective. Then it's your job to sell something. BTW, how'd you do on that test? That's OK, I don't test well either. But wait, there's more...

Now let's talk about writing a letter to a very different objective. How about creating a letter to keep a customer? A letter to build loyalty, trust, and friendship. Yes - all rolled up into a single sheet of paper. It's pretty easy to do, here's how: just write a thank you letter. "Thanks for your past business - I appreciate it." There, that wasn't so hard, was it? Instead of trying to sell something, take a minute out - spend the 41¢ on building a customer relationship. Use a letter so powerful it'll sit on a client's desk for a month: send a simple thank you. It'll be the best 41¢ you'll ever spend - and I guarantee it.

Let me ask you: When's the last time you received a thank you letter? That long ago, huh? No, I'm not talking about the pre-printed junk card your accountant bought from a catalog and sends you each year at Christmas. (OK, there go all the accountants calling their lawyers asking about a class action suit.) I'm talking about a real letter - one you've actually received from a real person, that said your name right there, up at the top, and continued, "thanks, thanks so much for your business this past year - I appreciate it."

Call me old fashioned, but I still believe it's a privilege to serve your customers. I'll bet they could go just about anywhere to buy services and products exactly like the ones you sell. But they don't - they get them from you. When's the last time you thanked them for that privilege? That long ago, too, huh? Do you know what other vendors call your best customers? They call them valuable prospects.

With a single thank you letter you can turn your best prospects into customers; you can encourage your best customers to do even more business with you, and feel better about doing it. Yes, they'll feel great about spending even more money with you - all from a single letter that was written with the objective of making them feel great about doing business with you. "Thanks for the business you give to us - we appreciate it. We're always ready with help, to answer your questions, and to assist you in any way we can, at any time. Thank you."

With two, well-written "Thanks for your business" letters, you can endear a person to remain your customer for years. You can plug that hole in the bottom of the customer bucket - you know, the one they keep falling out of.

And with three letters, with three thank you letters you can make a customer fall in love with you, your company, and they'll never even consider going anywhere else. Your letters need to say... oops, I'm out of room here - give me a call and I'll send you instructions for the third letter. Or call for an early look at my ramblings for next month on using letters.

Part II coming right up...

THE STRATEGIC USE OF LETTERS

In direct marketing, a letter is the absolute best marketing tool available at any price. Correction: giving away a new boat with a purchase is a better marketing tool. So let's say a letter is the best marketing tool you can use for under a dollar.

Letters can be used at every level: from prospecting, to turning prospects into customers, to securing sales, to CRM, to building brand and company loyalty, to creating a higher lifetime value of each customer. Just ask the insurance companies - you get a letter each year thanking you so much for all the money you spend with them, don't you? OK, perhaps we should phrase the question a little differently: Why do you suppose the insurance companies lose about one third of their clients each year - is it because they don't invest the 41¢ to send each customer a thank you letter each year? Yes, that's a better phrasing.

Letters can be targeted to one person, a broad field, an entire industry, an income group, or defined by geographics, demographics, psychographics, whatever. They can sell, position, generate a call, revive old customers, drive someone into your store or website, invoke just about any kind of response or just make someone feel great about doing business with you. All for just 41¢. Yep.

From personal pitches to classless advertisements with misspellings, a letter is a personal portrait of the sender.

Whether it's smooth and subtle or filled with typos, a letter is actually the most effective single piece of paper in all of direct marketing. Any arguments? Do you know what the most effective single sheet of paper is in all of marketing? I do. You'll have to email me for the answer, or just wait until next month's column.

A letter is like a reflective pool, showing the image of the sender through the circular ripples from just the slightest touch or the falling of a stray leaf. Wow, how profound. You didn't know us older folks still smoked pot, did you?

So, when you send a letter what kind of mark are you leaving in the business world? Is it crusty with jagged edges like my wife, or is it smooth and well researched like my secretary, carefully punctuated with a soft finesse. Does it have voluptuous curves and nice legs like her, too? Of course not... it's a letter - and every letter has it's limitations. Still, it can be most effective for bringing in additional business - even if it doesn't have silky auburn hair that drifts gently down her forehead when she looks at the computer, and every once in a while you can see her looking at you out of the corner of her eye.

How'd you make out with last months campaign? What - you haven't done it yet? Hurrmph. I'll make you a deal. Complete this campaign and if it doesn't work I'll send you a refund of all the money you paid for it. You do remember... last month we talked about the value of a letter campaign: 3 letters. (It was a short campaign.) You had promised me that right after watching Sponge Bob Square Pants that you were going to sit down and write 3 letters and send them to your top 100 prospects, and to your top 100 customers. Or, was that my kids promising they'd practice piano after watching...) Anyway, I'll make you this bet. Craft your letters well, and I'll bet it brings in business for you. Here's how.

First, you write your objective. We don't want to appear too sales-oriented with these letters, so we won't actually appear to sell anything in the first two letters. Our primary objectives will be to build a stronger customer relationship, increase customer retention, and build brand and company loyalty. Sales will follow naturally.

Here's the secret: the best way to meet our objectives is to thank our current customers for their past business. "Over the past several years I have had the privilege of serving you." Nope, sounds like a hooker quitting her job and leaving me a note on my dresser when she, um... I mean leaving her client a note on his dresser. But it's close.

How about, "Enclosed please find..." No, no, no! I hate that! Hey, if you've included it, they've already found it. You don't ever have to say that in a letter. As publishers, we send books to a lot of people. It's pretty superfluous for us to say in our letter, "We have enclosed our book..." No shit, they'd think, as they're holding our book weighting 2-1/2 pounds. It's the biggest thing in the box, dwarfing my letter that resting on top of it. Whatever your sending, I assure you they've found it just fine without your mentioning it. Well, at least I've never had anyone call and say, "Geeze, there was a book in the package? We couldn't find it."

So what do you say in our letter? "Thank you. Thank you so much for your business. I appreciate it. There are hundreds of places you can purchase goods and services similar to our's, but you buy them from us. So please accept my thanks, I really appreciate your business and your trust." Get the idea?

The second letter mentions the previous letter, in case they forgot. "In my last letter to you, I've tried to express just how much I appreciate the business you do with our firm." And then go on to sell some benefits; "I'm not sure I mentioned it, but there are some things you get with our firm you won't find in any of our brochures. First, you get our guarantee of complete satisfaction with every product you purchase from us. If you're not happy, we're not happy - and I encourage you to call me personally with any problems or questions as soon as they arise - so I can resolve any issues to your immediate and complete satisfaction. Next, you receive..."

Painting a picture of a firm everyone wants to do business with is easy in a letter. But like any promise, it's much easier to make than to keep. The third letter again, entices the customer with benefits, then at the end encourages the reader to call with the soft sell of, "We're here for you all day, every day. Please call me at any time to place an order, with questions, or with your comments about our products or services. I'm always as close as your phone. If you need me after hours, here's my personal cell phone number:" P.S. It's OK to turn your phone off after work - if it's that important, they'll call you first thing the next morning.

Part III on next page...

THE MOST EFFECTIVE SINGLE SHEET OF PAPER IN ALL OF MARKETING IS...

So the last couple of articles you've heard me gripe about how you should send more letters. Yip yip yip yip yip. Send more letters, send more letters. I sound like your mother when she told you not to get that tattoo, don't I? And you're still sorry you got it, aren't you?

Well, here's the reason: letters are great marketing tools. You can reach anyone with a letter - the president of a bank or of an airline, a top executive of almost any corporation, or the purchasing agent who buys your goods or services. While prospecting for new business, I'll admit that giving customers a new car carries considerably more weight, but in most cases a simple letter works just fine for making the phone ring.

I consistently and respectfully remind my own clients of the value of the printed word when sent - one page at a time - to a specific prospect or customer. But do they listen? If a tree falls in the forest does anyone care?

A letter is the most effective single sheet of paper in direct marketing, but it is not the most effective single sheet of paper in all of marketing. That, my friend, would be a hundred dollar bill. Ooops, excuse me, that's the most important single sheet of paper when you get pulled over by a cop for speeding.

In marketing, the most important single page you can create is... is... I'm building suspense... is... a press release. If you knew that, kindly raise your right hand. Hey, you in the back - raise your other right hand. Now, if you send a press release out every two months, raise your left hand. Have both of your hands raised high in the air? OK, now gimme all your money, this is a stick-up.

If you don't have both your hands raised, take note: you're making a big mistake, unless of course you don't want any more money. So, you're maxed out - running your business three or four shifts a day? I know the feeling - it's rough, isn't it - trying to spend all that extra money to avoid all those additional taxes. If this is the case, you shouldn't be sending out press releases every couple of months, you should be sending some of that additional money to me.

As a marketing guy, I feel everyone can use more business - at least that's why people call me. And when they do I tell them they need to send out more letters... and more press releases. There - I saved you a ton of money. Just send me $500 and I'll wave the rest of my invoice for now. Press releases and letter campaigns are two of the lowest cost ways to promote any business.

For the price of a couple of sheets of paper - a press release and a cover letter - you can generate a story about your firm that will be published in newspapers and magazines. It's easy, at least in theory.

For the price of a couple of beers - your wife and a good, ahem, woman friend, you can generate a story about you that will be published in newspapers and magazines, too. It would be in a different section. But, we'll save that for another article.

A press release is a one-page, double spaced document about you, your firm, its products or services, with a compelling headline and a story written in a brief, pyramid-style (the important stuff at the top) news format.

When writing a press release, start with the MOST important element as the headline. Here's where I differ from most PR agencies: strangely enough I recommend that in the first two lines of your body copy you weave in one or two of the biggest benefits of your products, or of doing business with your firm. People buy from the benefits, so it's important to show readers what your's are. Stating your benefits this early in the release ensures they won't get edited out: editors traditionally cut from the bottom of the release. Immediately after the benefits, present the rest of the facts in their descending order of relevance. I call this the "benefits-first" press release.

Compare your press release (also called a news release) to a newspaper story which features the most important event in the headline: for example, "Fire Kills 3!" The story unfolds with facts in a descending order of importance, "At 123 Maple Ave... a six alarm fire... blah, blah, blah... 30 firemen where called... blah, blah, blah... neighbors watched..." spiraling down to the trailing end of the story, "368 donuts were eaten by the police and firemen..."

When your press release is written in a tight, crisp news-style format: who, what, where, when, how, without filler or fluff - the chance of it being published in a newspaper or magazine are much greater. 20% in small papers and trade magazines, 5% in larger papers, less than 1% in the larger consumer magazines.

If you call the editor it can double the chances your story will run. If the editor is cranky when you speak with him or her, be brief, and tell them it was nice speaking to them even though it wasn't. If they're on-deadline and don't answer their phone, leave a competitor's name on their voice mail, tell them it was urgent, leave a 6 digit phone number while crinkling a Tastykake Creamies wrapper in the mouthpiece of the phone to sound like static. Hey, remember when you got 2 Creamies in a package - now they just give you one big one shaped like two stuck together and hope you don't notice. So, you're that old, too?

If published, your story appears as editorial, alongside the rest of the manufactured news and other generated-news pieces. Over 50% of the stories in a newspaper, outside of the first few pages which are considered "hard news" are generated by press releases.

There are lots of ways to spin a business story, and lots of ways to get media attention and ink, but I always create newspaper pitches with a human interest story line and a very strong headline. Press releases for magazine or for the business section of papers can be more product or company oriented. If the headline doesn't make potential customers read the story, why bother? If you have a piece about your firm printed in The Wall Street Journal but no one calls, what good did it do you?

A good way to come up with a strong headline is the Jeff Dobkin 100 to 1 Rule: Write 100 headlines, then go back and pick our your best one. I didn't say you'd like it, I just said it was a good way. You can find the full article titled "The 100 to 1 Rule" in my book, Uncommon Marketing Techniques.

Here are two main headline formula I use quite a bit: One headline is for product marketing: "New Product Offers Benefit," (example: "New Lawnmower is Easier to Push"). The other headline formula is for getting quality leads by offering a FREE booklet. Use a title that drives only real customers to call, to save you time and stop wasting your expensive literature. Example: "Free booklet: How To get this Benefit" ("Free Booklet: How to Stop Leaks in Older Roofs"). If you were a roofer, this would be the perfect press release headline - editors love to have free things sent to their readers so there's a good chance your release would be published, and guess who would call you? I would. You'd owe me the other $500 for this lesson.

I couldn't help but include this theory I have about saving lives. You see, the rest of the book may save you money, but this may save your life, or the life of your child or a friend. If you remember only one detail from this entire book, I hope this is it. As with all my writing, your comments and questions are most welcome. If you ever employ this technique, please call me and let me know that my life's work has been successful in saving a human life. Thank you. For the longer version of this technique, along with its history, please see the book Successful, Low Cost Marketing Methods. *Thanks.* THEORY BY JEFFREY DOBKIN •

A TECHNIQUE FOR DELAYING BRAIN DEATH IN HEART ATTACK VICTIMS

WHILE CURRENT MEDICAL METHODS cannot entirely prevent heart attacks, there is an emergency procedure that can save lives. A simple technique can reduce or delay the possibility of brain damage and brain death to a heart attack victim for up to an hour—or more.

If this procedure saves one life, it is fully worth all the time and effort I have spent in research.

The Technique seeks to prevent or delay the irreversible brain damage thought to occur when no oxygen reaches the brain for four minutes.[1] It is used as a time-buying procedure to save the lives of heart attack victims and victims of suffocation, drowning, respiratory failure, and drug overdose. Perhaps it will even help SIDS (crib death) or stroke victims until proper medical equipment and personnel are summoned and arrive.

The Technique can be applied by a child or may be self-administered in almost any home. It takes less than 30 seconds to initiate and the results are as immediate.[2] It works on both conscious and unconscious victims. It can be explained on the phone in under a minute.

Almost everyone has heard of a boy drowning in cold water—then, after half an hour of submersion, being resuscitated with no ill effects and no brain damage. The *Canadian Medical Association Journal* documented such a drowning: After half an hour of complete submersion, a boy was rescued from the icy waters where he fell.[3] He was resuscitated and, with proper medical treatment, had no lasting side effects. There was no cerebral damage, although his brain received no oxygen for over half an hour.

Research has provided additional case study after case study of extended cold water submersion with no brain damage to resuscitated victims. Article after article, story after story, of people deprived of oxygen for up to an hour—with no ill effects or brain damage. What is it that protects the brain from damage in cases of oxygen deprivation over the four-minute limit? And can this be applied as a lifesaving technique to heart attack victims?

In all vertebrates, there is an automatic reflex called the Mammalian Diving Reflex. It occurs naturally as a life-preserving mechanism during cold water submersion. More commonly called the "Diving Reflex," it is a protective oxygen-conserving reflex to keep brain and body alive during submergence and possible drowning in cold water. The body prepares itself to sustain life. It is a totally natural protective mechanism serving Homo sapiens, originating from hundreds of thousands of years of evolvement.

Natural engagement of the diving reflex is what has enabled drowning victims to be revived successfully after cold water submersion for as long as an hour, with few or no ill effects. The Technique seeks to trigger this reflex in a crisis. The Technique may never replace CPR. The purpose of this article is not to compete with CPR, but to help sustain the life of the hundreds of thousands of victims of heart attacks or suffocation, thrust into a life-and-death situation, who may not be near people trained in CPR.

If you are not skilled in CPR, and you live in the country where an ambulance is 20 minutes away, and someone close to you has a heart attack—the options are frightening. Without the initiation of the Technique, a person whose heart stops has only four minutes until irreversible brain damage occurs. After you call for help, you can watch. If you think this is a horrifying alternative, I couldn't agree more. Or you can try this Technique.

The Technique may work to save lives in conjunction with CPR. There is also the possibility it may not work at all; this is, after all, a theory. But the fact that it just may work makes it worth closer study. When there is no other immediate remedy, this may be put into practice in an emergency. What would you have your spouse do if you lived in the country and you had a heart attack?

"The Technique for Delaying Brain Damage" is simple and easy to initiate. In natural surroundings, the diving reflex occurs when a mammal falls into water 58 degrees Fahrenheit—the mean temperature of the waters of the world—or colder. But this reflex may also be triggered by only a facial immersion in cold water (58 degrees or colder). **The Technique is to apply cold water, wet towels, or wet ice packs to the victim's face—especially the eyes—to trigger the diving reflex in the event of heart or respiratory failure.** This procedure starts the oxygen-conserving mammalian diving reflex. Here is what happens:

Bradycardia can start in as little as four seconds or can take up to thirty seconds, depending on what part of the breath cycle the person is in when cold water is applied to the face. In man, cold water facial immersion usually induces a 15% to 30% decrease in heart rate from normal resting values. The reflex is strong enough to override other seemingly vital reflexes; i.e., it can completely obliterate the tachycardia that accompanies moderately severe exercise on a bicycle ergometer and can abruptly reduce heart rate from 130–140 beats per minute to 80 or less, despite continuation of the exercise.[4] Bradycardia is initiated by parasympathetic vagal activity.

Skin and muscle blood flow decrease through a powerful constriction of peripheral arteries. Peripheral vaso-constriction brought about by sympathetic activity maintains blood pressure. At the same time, systemic arterial pressure, especially diastolic, is increased. This lower heart rate and redistribution of central blood flow supports more necessary life-preserving organs.

The reflex triggers anaerobic metabolism, shown by a fall in arterial pH. There is an increase in concentrations of lactic and other organic acids, and a rise in blood carbon dioxide and potassium. This indicates that the body's cells are using less oxygen.

In a study by Wolf, Schneider and Groover, arterial oxygen saturation fell very little during immersion when the reflex occured.[5]

Because arterial oxygen saturation falls very little, the term "oxygen conserving" is appropriate for the reflex—an animal is enabled to survive without breathing for a much longer period than its supply of oxygen would warrant under ordinary circumstances.[6]

In Diving Reflex experiments, Charles Richet tied off the tracheae of two groups of ducks, then held one group under cold water. The ducks held under water lived more than three times as long as their partners not immersed in cold water.

In further studies of nerve-cutting experiments, Harold Anderson of Oslo, Norway, documented that the Diving Reflex, as manifested by slowing of the heart, depended on the integrity of the ophthalmic branch of the trigeminal nerve. With the nerve intact, a duck would trigger the diving reflex and survive under water for 20 minutes. When the ophthalmic branch of the trigeminal nerve was severed (bilaterally), immersed ducks failed to slow their heart rates when cold water was applied to their faces and survived only six or seven minutes.[7]

Accentuation of the reflex to the greatest degree occurs when the facial immersion in cold water is accompanied by fear. The more fearful the condition, the stronger the trigger to bring about the reflex and the greater the chance a strong oxygen-conserving reflex will take place.

In patients resuscitated by the team of a special ambulance service run by the Department of Anesthesia at Ulleval Hospital (from an article entitled "Resuscitation of Drowning Victims"), the most successful outcome was observed in those with cardiac arrest following drowning.

In an article in *Newsweek,* drowning specialist Dr. Martin J. Nemiroff (Michigan University Medical Center) suggests that the involuntary diving reflex saves lives of drowning victims by delaying suffocation—by shunting oxygen from extremities and sending it toward the heart, brain, and lungs—and reduces the possibility of brain damage and death.[8] A photo in the *Newsweek* article shows Dr. Nemiroff with Brian Cunningham, who was revived after 38 minutes under water.

Dr. Nemiroff has successfully revived numerous victims of cold water drowning who were submerged for 30 minutes or more and were pronounced dead. He says that what saved the victims was the automatic activation of the Mammalian Diving Reflex and the coldness of the water.[9]

It is my conclusion that if the diving reflex can save the lives of drowning victims by delaying brain damage, then triggering the reflex should also delay brain damage in heart attack victims.

A discussion in a *Scientific American* study of the human body's ability to resist drowning states that the Diving Reflex and cold water reduce the oxygen demand of tissues, extending the period of survival without external oxygen to as long as one hour. Previously, irreversible brain damage was thought to occur after four minutes without oxygen.[10]

The Diving Reflex is currently used by the medical profession in conversion of paroxysmal atrial tachycardia.[11,12,13] The Technique is to immerse the face of a person in a tub or basin of water 50 degrees or cooler. Since the technique produces an almost instant conversion to normal sinus rhythm and is not invasive, the use of the Diving Reflex is recommended by many authors and cited as a safe, effective treatment. In one study, nine out of 10 patients converted in 15–38 seconds, with an average of 23 seconds.[14] Its use is also the treatment of choice for converting a supraventricular tachycardia in children and infants, in whom the Diving Reflex effect is most pronounced.[15]

In a letter to Mr. Dobkin, Dr. Linus Pauling surmises there are two ways in which the damage to the brain might be delayed for some time when the oxygen to the blood is stopped.

"The brain can tolerate a certain amount of decrease in the partial pressure of oxygen supplied by the blood. If the circulation of the blood to the brain and to the tissues continues at its normal rate, the oxygen is used up rather fast, most of it (75%) by tissues other than the brain. Accordingly the induction of bradycardia, delaying the rate at which oxygen is brought to the tissues by the blood, would conserve the supply of oxygen and permit anoxic damage to be delayed by a considerable amount.

"There is a second way of delaying brain damage by anoxia. This way is to cool the brain. The biochemical reactions involved in anoxic damage have a high temperature coefficient, so that cooling the brain by a few degrees can slow down the rate at which anoxic damage occurs to perhaps one-tenth of its rate."[16] This letter suggests that ice or cold water also be applied to the neck, so that the blood is cooled and the brain itself is cooled in the region in which anoxic damage occurs. I concur with Dr. Pauling and recommend that after the face is immersed with ice packs or cold water, cold water be applied to the neck and the base of the hairline at the back of the head.

After countless hours of research, I am convinced that the Technique to delay brain damage will save lives. The technique of applying cold water to the face of conscious or unconscious heart attack or suffocation victims should be a known lifesaving procedure. It may be used in the event of any oxygen deprivation to the brain. Its procedure can be explained over the telephone, self-administered, or applied by a friend or child with no training. And while it will not stop heart attacks from happening, it will buy precious time until proper medical equipment and personnel arrive.

The Technique is quick and easy to apply. It is a time-buying procedure—when time is of the essence. It is nature's own way of protecting us—a non-invasive action that can be initiated immediately by someone with no training. This natural, life-conserving reflex is common enough to be found in all mammals and powerful enough to save someone's life in a traumatic moment.

Further investigation and clinical evaluation may be necessary, but from the empirical evidence I have uncovered, I recommend this reflex be initiated in time of emergent need. I hope this article is a catalyst to spur new research. My reward? I would like my name assigned to the Technique; after all, Heimlich has his maneuver. My goal? I hope at least one life is saved.

The Dobkin Technique triggers nature's own protective oxygen-saving mechanism to save lives. It is the same reflex that has saved children and adults from drowning even though they were completely submerged in cold water for up to an hour. Your comments are most welcome. If you know someone who has been revived from a cold water drowning, please write to me. Also, if this technique has been used, please let me know the details. Thank you.

Jeffrey Warren Dobkin • P.O. Box 100 • Merion Station, PA 19066

Abstract References:

CPR, Diving Reflex, Heart Attack, Brain Damage, SIDS, Suffocation, Respiratory Failure.

IMPORTANT: Please email this abstract to everyone you can think of - it may save someone's life.

~ Abstract ~

Help for heart attack victims—when no one is around who knows CPR, initiate "The Dobkin Technique for Delaying Brain Death": Apply cold water or cold wet towels (58 degrees or colder) to the face and eyes of victim—leaving nose and mouth clear to breathe. After this, supplemental help may be to apply additional cold wet cloths to the base of the back of the head and to the back of the neck. This is an emergency time-buying procedure to delay brain death by triggering the Diving Reflex. The Diving Reflex is a natural oxygen-conserving reflex which can delay the irreversible brain damage thought to occur within four minutes of oxygen deprivation. Works on conscious and unconscious victims; may be applied by child or self-administered; technique may be described over the phone. Works in under 30 seconds. Works in both adult and children, victims of suffocation, SIDS, drownings, drug overdose, choking, electrocution, and other victims of respiratory failure or deprivation of oxygen for any reason.

Endnotes

1. *Scientific American*, August 1977, 57.

2. S. Wolf, R.A. Schneider, and M.E. Groover, "Further Studies on the Circulatory and Metabolic Alterations of the Oxygen-Conserving (Diving) Reflex in Man," (paper presented before the American Clinical and Climatological Association, Colorado Springs, Colo., 21 October 1964).

3. P.K. Hunt, "Effect and Treatment of the Diving Reflex," *Canadian Medical Association Journal* (21 December 1974).

4. J. Atkins, S. Leshin, C. Skelton, and K. Widenthal, "The Diving Reflex Used to Treat Paroxysmal Atrial Tachycardia," *Lancet* (4 January 1975): 12.

5. Wolf et al., "Further Studies."

6. Ibid.

7. Ibid.

8. *Newsweek*, 22 August 1977, 79.

9. *New York Times,* 7 August 1977, 20.

10. *Scientific American,* August 1977, 57.

11. Atkins et al., "Diving Reflex," 12.

12. *Newsweek,* 13 January 1975, 50.

13. P.G. Landsberg, "Bradycardia During Human Diving," *South African Medical Journal* (5 April 1975): 626-630.

14. M.A. Wayne, "Conversion of Paroxysmal Atrial Tachycardia by Facial Immersion in Ice Water," *Journal of the American College of Emergency Physicians* (6 May 1976).

15. V. Whitman, "The Diving Reflex in Termination of Supraventricular Tachycardia in Childhood," *Journal of the American College of Emergency Physicians,* letter to the editor (December 1976).

16. Letter to Jeffrey Dobkin from Dr. Linus Pauling, dated September 2, 1992.

Copyright Permission: Permission is hereby granted to use the writing of this technique to delay brain damage in whole or in part to save lives, or to increase the public awareness of this technique as a lifesaving emergency procedure—as long as credit is given to Jeffrey Dobkin and the technique referred to as "The Dobkin Technique" for Delaying Brain Death.

Additional Services from
The Danielle Adams Publishing Company

Package Review
30-minute audio (on cassette) or handwritten corrections of your package. Includes suggestions and direction.

Package Analysis
Deeper package analysis (or review of longer packages) along with additional marketing analysis and instruction.

Market Analysis and Consulting
Two-hour market analysis package. Includes live discussion of your current marketing and suggestions and recommendations on where and how to move forward quickly, at low cost.

Consulting
Marketing, advertising, direct marketing, catalog review, new product development, resources, direction. Fresh, objective views. Jeffrey is quite used to saving clients way more than they spend on his services. On site, or printed or web work on the phone.

Writing
Retail, catalog copy, direct mail, and technical writing, too. Market action plans. Ad copy - including direct-selling ads. Business letters a specialty. Marketing campaigns. Press releases that work, and letters that go with them. Traditional and direct response copywriting that make your phone ring. Manuals, instructions, books, annual reports, and ghostwriting - you'd be surprised at whom Jeffrey writes for. Radio and television commercials and scripts.

Traditional Advertising
Ads, brochures, (design and copywriting), collateral material, business graphics, logos and logo enhancements, from the master of graphics himself. TV and radio commercials - consulting, writing, and scripting, directing. Worldwide.

Direct Marketing
Letters are a specialty. Direct mail copywriting, and direct marketing letters, brochures, packages. Also, finding markets, list analysis, magazine analysis, Ad placement. Market analysis, Writing and graphics for direct selling ads, consulting. Please call for additional information and pricing.

Speaking
When Jeffrey Dobkin speaks, people laugh. They also listen & learn. Like his books, Jeff crams a lot of useful information into a presentation. Call for information.
~ Telephone 610-642-1000 ~

BOOKS

THEY'RE EVERYTHING
YOU'VE EVER IMAGINED...
AND MORE!

DANIELLE ADAMS
PUBLISHING COMPANY

> ## As with all our publications, we hope you've enjoyed this book and found it of great value.

Disclaimer: We are not responsible for anything.

The opinions in this text are not necessarily those of the publisher, or the author. We don't really know whose opinions they are, and please see disclaimer above. Wow. You know, we really didn't think you'd call us on it, and read this stuff here in the back in tiny print.

Addendum to Disclaimer. By reading this text you agree to our 42 page agreement contract found on page 714 of our website, just like when you sign up for any mobile phone service or install any computer software. And this call is being recorded to bring you better service... like recording the call had anything to do with bringing you better service. If we really wanted to bring you better service, we wouldn't record this call, and we'd have gotten rid of voice mail and answered the phone ourselves. Anyhow, if you find a typo or misspelling in this book, and we intentionally left a few in so you'd have something to point out to others, yea, like you never had a typo in something you wrote, we appreciate your telling us so we can correct it in future editions. If you don't, it can no longer be considered our fault - we took a shot and spelled it the best way we could at the time. This policy falls in nicely with our disclaimer as stated above. We asked the writer to spell everything correctly and he replied "If you only have one way to spell a word, you're not really a man, are you?" That would explain the several different spellings of the same word in different chapters. Plus, try as we might, some stuff just gets out. We know you're not one of those really picky people who would hold it against us, are you? While you're standing there not doing anything, please take this book up to the cash register and purchase it. Thanks for buying this book. Or, as an alternative, just send us the money. Thank you.

We actually had a lot more to say, a lot more - so we put it in another book: *The Ten Best In Direct Marketing*. But we needed a couple of more pages in this one to make it look bigger.

Yep.

Speaking, Jeffrey Dobkin:

Speaking, Seminars, & Presentations, Jeffrey Dobkin

If you're looking for a an explosive speaker – one that captivates the attention of an audience, tells stale jokes but who cares—they're still funny, yet provides enough information that attendees actually take notes and go back and use the stuff he says to increase their response and make the phone ring – this looks like a job for Superman. But, he's probably busy. So give Jeff Dobkin a call at 610-642-1000 and talk to him. He does a swell job at supplying practical, useful direct marketing information in a fun way.

If you aren't looking for lean, nuts and bolts "How-To" marketing information, hey, please go back and find out what you're doing that's so right that you don't need help in getting additional sales leads and phone calls and if you really do already have all the business and money you can handle – then call us and let us know. We'd love to pass those tips on to others. PS – if you do this by working 18 hours a day, forget it. Anyone can do it like that. We all have wives and kids we can't wait to get away from also, but is working 18 hours a day the way to do it? I say we balance our work day – work 1/2 day, then go for lunch... umm, a long lunch. Nice balance, isn't it? See further instructions at www.dobkin.com.

As you can probably surmise from this book, Dobkin's presentations are fun and funny, but still the information is rich and in good depth. "I realize the subject is marketing, but first and foremost I believe a speaker needs to be entertaining. I make a dry subject come alive with humorous stories and good natured stale jokes throughout. All the while I place a heavy accent on practical, useful marketing information." says Dobkin in a more sober moment. Or is that somber moment? Call 610-642-1000 for information or to speak to a booking agent.

Consulting, Jeff Dobkin:

Dobkin is our featured writer, chief marketer, and a pretty darned good consultant at fixing a marketing plan, writing new marketing plans and making any firm's marketing more cost-effective. We rent him out for commercial writing assignments too: letters, brochures, collateral, direct marketing material, all phases of TV and radio commercials, catalog copy and so forth. On a serious note we unleash him to write marketing plans and promotional plans. Dobkin also does consulting in business strategy, promotional marketing and direct marketing. Missing sales? Need more sales at less cost? Give him a call.

When I asked him why his marketing is better than most everyone else's marketing he told me this: "After 25 years, I've gone into thousands of firms and asked, "What's working in your marketing? What isn't? So now I have a pretty good idea of what works for most businesses—at just about every budget. I can spot a hole in a marketing campaign from a mile away, and tell you what you need in a short time, especially if you have gaping inadequacies in your marketing strategies, as most firms do." He's helpful - and really quite amazing, really - at consulting. The stuff he comes up with - even in the first meeting is incredible. He's amazing with start-ups, working with inventors and inventions and an expert in larger firms traditional and untraditional marketing. He simply knows how and when to break the rules.

For years Dobkin has read every marketing book and magazine he could, and now his articles on marketing have been featured in over 250 magazines, including just about every marketing and direct marketing magazine published.

It all starts with a phone call: 610-642-1000 rings on his desk. Initial calls are always at no charge - go on, see what he has to say about what you're doing. If it's right, he'll confirm it. If it's wrong - or needs a correction, you'll learn that too. 610-642-1000. Thanks and we hope you enjoyed this book.

How To Market a Product for Under $500

Just $39.95 + $5 P&H for a signed edition.

An older title that is now a cult classic, a real one-of-a-kind book on marketing. The depth of information is incredible in this practical and useful marketing tool. Over 25,000 copies in print - 5 press runs in over 15 years. Now, this book has now been updated to its new title, *Successful Low Cost Marketing Methods ($24.95+$5)*, but you can get the original cult title by ordering it right here.

Uncommon Marketing Techniques

Still Just $17.95 + $4 P&H. 35 articles. Order directly from our offices and we send them officially Signed by Jeff. This title is available instantly online by E-Book.

Direct Marketing Strategies

25 more articles just like the ones you read - but better! Hey, just kidding. But if you liked this book, Jeff's conversational style, and the wealth of practical marketing techniques he presents, please consider buying our other titles including *Direct Marketing Strategies*, we need the money. Just $17.95 +$4 P&H - Thanks. E-Book available.

The Intelligent Testing System

10 Auido Cassettes written and narrated by Jeffrey + 2 hugh binders of marketing material and reference data (400 + Pages). Shows you how to market through classified ads and direct mail. Please see our website or request our FREE brochure. Just $299.95 + $12 (ships at over ten pounds!). Introductory Booklet, $14.95 +$3

Audio CDs From The Danielle Adams Publishing Company

60 Ideas/Direct Marketing 1 hour.
Hear Jeff in a Live - and Lively Presentation. Just $29.95 +$4

How To Buy a Great Mailing List. 1 Hour, Direct Marketing Guru Markus Allen interviews Jeff. In studio. $29.95 +$4

Radio Show with Jeff Dobkin, "11 Tips for Retailers" :40 Minutes. Just $19.95 + $4

Radio Show: "10 Ways to Thank Customers" Just $14.95 +$4

Notes... Comments, Or Questions.

If you have any, write them on this page, send or fax them to us, and Jeffrey will be happy to respond. If you want, you can give us the right to publish this material with your approval.

Print Name_____ Phone_____

You can also email Jeffrey directly at Jeff@Dobkin.com COMMENTS:

___Yes! Please Rush Me the Following:

_____

_____

_____

Send Check, Money Order, or Call to Charge to Visa/MC, Discover, or AMEX.

Name_____

Address_____

City, St_____Zip_____

Telephone_____Fax_____

Products_____Quantity

Credit Card Number

_____Exp_____

Signature_____Amount_____ Thank you!

For additional orders, photocopy this form or just use a sheet of paper.

THE DANIELLE ADAMS PUBLISHING CO.
~ *Satisfaction Always Guaranteed* ~
BOX 100 ✫ MERION STATION, PA 19066
610/642-1000 ✫ FAX 610/642-6832
ORDERS: 800/234-IDEA